Introduction

This revision guide covers the EDEXCEL GCSE MATHEMATICS: SPECIFICATION A (1387) and as such is matched meticulously to this specification. Everything you need to know is contained within this guide, but just as importantly, there is no superfluous material.

The contributors to this guide are former or current GCSE examiners and have used their considerable experience to produce clear, easy to follow explanations and exam style examples laid out in columnar form to reduce line length and improve readability.

Ideally this guide should be used with its associated workbook to provide a superb GCSE resource at an unbelievable price. Each page of the workbook matches the revision guide page for page and consists of structured questions with spaces for answers, plus extension questions. Details of the workbook and our other mathematics guides can be found on the back and inside cover.

Consultant Editor:
John Proctor B.Sc. (Hons), Cert. Ed.
Director of Specialist College,
St. Mary's Catholic High School,
Astley,
Manchester
(An 11-18 Specialist Mathematics and Computing College)

Proofreader:
Kay Chawner
Formerly a mathematics teacher at The Ridgeway School, Swindon.

*Although this guide is intended for candidates following the linear specification, it can also be used by candidates following the MODULAR B (1388) specification.

Contents

Number

- 4 Place Value
- 5 Numbers 1
- 6 Numbers 2
- 7 Integers 1
- 8 Integers 2
- 9 Order of Operations
- 10 Rounding Numbers 1
- 11 Rounding Numbers 2
- 12 Estimating & Checking
- 13 Powers and Roots
- 14 Fractions 1
- 15 Fractions 2
- 16 Fractions 3
- 17 Calculations Involving Fractions
- 18 Decimals 1
- 19 Decimals 2
- 20 Multiplication of Decimals
- 21 Division of Decimals
- 22 Percentages 1
- 23 Percentages 2
- 24 Percentages 3
- 25 Converting Between Systems
- 26 Everyday Maths 1
- 27 Everyday Maths 2
- 28 Ratio and Proportion 1
- 29 Ratio and Proportion 2

Algebra

- 30 The Basics of Algebra
- 31 Substitution
- 32 Brackets and Factorisation
- 33 Solving Linear Equations 1
- 34 Solving Linear Equations 2
- 35 Formulae 1
- 36 Formulae 2
- 37 Number Patterns & Sequences
- 38 Plotting Points
- 39 Graphs of Linear Functions 1
- 40 Graphs of Linear Functions 2
- 41 Other Graphs 1
- 42 Other Graphs 2
- 43 Other Graphs 3

Shape, Space and Measures

- 44 Angles 1
- 45 Angles 2
- 46 Triangles
- 47 Types of Triangle
- 48 Quadrilaterals
- 49 Irregular Polygons
- 50 Regular Polygons
- 51 Congruence and Tessellation
- 52 Similarity
- 53 Transformations 1
- 54 Transformations 2
- 55 Transformations 3
- 56 Transformations 4
- 57 Coordinates 1
- 58 Coordinates 2
- 59 Perimeter 1
- 60 Perimeter 2
- 61 Area 1
- 62 Area 2
- 63 Area 3
- 64 Volume
- 65 3-D Shapes 1
- 66 3-D Shapes 2
- 67 Symmetry 1
- 68 Symmetry 2
- 69 Scale Drawings & Map Scales
- 70 Measuring Bearings
- 71 Reading Scales
- 72 Converting Measurements
- 73 Speed
- 74 Constructions 1
- 75 Constructions 2
- 76 Properties of Circles

Handling Data

- 77 Probability
- 78 Mutually Exclusive Outcomes
- 79 Listing All Outcomes
- 80 Estimated Probability
- 81 Collecting Data 1
- 82 Collecting Data 2
- 83 Sorting Data 1
- 84 Sorting Data 2
- 85 Sorting Data 3
- 86 Displaying Data 1
- 87 Displaying Data 2
- 88 Scatter Diagrams 1
- 89 Scatter Diagrams 2
- 90 Pie Charts
- 91 Mean, Median, Mode & Range 1
- 92 Mean, Median, Mode & Range 2
- 94 Using a Scientific Calculator 1
- 95 Using a Scientific Calculator 2
- 96 Index

Place Value

Place Value in Whole Numbers

The value of a digit in a whole number depends on its position in the number. This is called its place value (see the table below). The table below can easily be extended to include ten thousands, hundred thousands, millions etc. This means that it does not matter how large a number is, each digit will still have a place value.

Place Value of Digits				Number
1 000 Thousands	100 Hundreds	10 Tens	1 Units	
			7	Seven
		4	2	Forty two
	6	5	9	Six hundred and fifty nine
3	1	8	5	Three thousand, one hundred and eighty five

Rounding Numbers

Numbers can be very large and often these numbers make more sense if they are rounded to a given power of 10 e.g. 10 (10^1), 100 (10^2), 1 000 (10^3). Let's take the attendance at a football match. The actual attendance is 38 726. However to a neutral observer an attendance figure to the nearest thousand would have more meaning. Look at the place value table below which shows this attendance.

The digit to the right of the one you are working to will tell you if you need to round up. For example, when rounding a number to the nearest thousand you need to look at the digit in the hundreds column. If it is 5 or more, the digit in the thousands column is **rounded up**. If it is 4 or less the digit in the thousands column **stays the same**. The digits in the hundreds, tens and units columns become zero, showing the number to the nearest 1 000.

10 000 Ten Thousands	1 000 Thousands	100 Hundreds	10 Tens	1 Units
3	8	7	2	6
3	9	0	0	0
3	8	7	0	0
3	8	7	3	0

Nearest 1 000: Round up

Nearest 100: Stays the same

Nearest 10: Round up

Numbers 1

Types of Number

Numbers can be described in many ways. Below is a summary of the types of number that you should know.

Even Numbers

These are numbers which can be divided exactly by 2. The first ten even numbers in order are ...

2, 4, 6, 8, 10, 12, 14, 16, 18, 20

Odd Numbers

Since all whole numbers are either even or odd then odd numbers are those that cannot be divided exactly by 2. The first ten odd numbers in order are ...

1, 3, 5, 7, 9, 11, 13, 15, 17, 19

Factors

The factors of a number are those whole numbers which divide exactly into it. All numbers (with the exception of square numbers, see page 13) have an even number of factors. An easy way to find the factors of a number is to choose pairs of numbers which multiply to give that number. For example...

The factors of **10** are **1, 2, 5, 10**
(since 1 x 10 = 10, 2 x 5 =10)
The factors of **24** are **1, 2, 3, 4, 6, 8, 12, 24**
(since 1 x 24 = 24, 2 x 12 =24, 3 x 8 = 24, 4 x 6 = 24)

As we said, square numbers have an odd number of factors, for example...

The factors of **16** are **1, 2, 4, 8, 16**
(since 1 x 16 = 16, 2 x 8 =16, 4 x 4 = 16)
The factors of **36** are
1, 2, 3, 4, 6, 9, 12, 18, 36
(since 1 x 36 = 36, 2 x 18 = 36,
3 x 12 = 36, 4 x 9 = 36, 6 x 6 = 36)

Multiples

The multiples of a number are those numbers which can be divided exactly by it. To put it simply, they are the numbers found in the 'times' tables.

The multiples of **5** are
5, 10, 15, 20, 25 and so on...

The multiples of **8** are
8, 16, 24, 32, 40 and so on...

Common Factors

These are whole numbers which will divide exactly into more than one other whole number. For example ...

Factors of 10 are 2 and 5.
Factors of 15 are 3 and 5.

Therefore **5** is a common factor of **10** and **15** (and also a lot of other numbers divisible by 5!!)

Reciprocals

The reciprocal of a number is simply '1 over that number', for example...

- the reciprocal of 4 is '1 over 4' = $\frac{1}{4}$

- the reciprocal of 0.2 is '1 over 0.2'
  = $\frac{1}{0.2} = \frac{10}{2} = 5$ (x10)

- the reciprocal of $\frac{2}{3}$ is '1 over $\frac{2}{3}$'
  = $\frac{1}{\frac{2}{3}} = 1 \div \frac{2}{3} = 1 \times \frac{3}{2} = \frac{3}{2} = 1\frac{1}{2}$

Numbers 2

Addition and Subtraction of Whole Numbers

Whenever you add or subtract whole numbers you must line up the digits, one on top of the other, in place value order.

Examples...

1 356 + 72

```
  356
+  72
 ----
  428
```

- Start from the right hand side.
- 6 + 2 = 8. Put 8 down.
- 5 + 7 = 12. Put 2 down and carry 1.
- 3 + 1 = 4. Put 4 down.

2 438 - 57

```
  438
-  57
 ----
  381
```

- Start from the right hand side.
- 8 - 7 = 1. Put 1 down.
- 3 - 5 doesn't work. Borrow 1 from the hundreds column to give 13 - 5 = 8. Put 8 down.
- 3 - 0 = 3. Put 3 down.

Long Multiplication and Long Division of Whole Numbers

To be successful at long multiplication and long division you need to know the multiplication or 'times' tables.

Examples...

1 364 x 14

```
   364
 x  14
 -----
  3640
  1456
 -----
  5096
```

- 14 = 10 + 4.
- Do the 364 x 10 first. Remember to put a '0' down as you would if you multiplied any whole number by 10.
- Do the 364 x 4 multiplication.
- Add the two multiplications together.

Examples continued ...

2 312 ÷ 12

```
      26
   -----
 12)312
     24
     --
     72
     72
     --
      0
```

- 12 does not divide into 3 so move on.
- 12 into 31 goes 2 times. 12 x 2 = 24. Write 24 below 31 and subtract to give 7.
- Bring down the 2. 12 into 72 goes 6 times. 12 x 6 = 72.

Multiplication and Division of Whole Numbers by Powers of 10

To multiply a whole number by a power of 10 e.g. $10(10^1)$, $100(10^2)$, $1\,000(10^3)$ all you have to do is move all the digits a certain number of place values to the left, as determined by the power. When you do this your number becomes bigger, for example...

1 36 x 10 = 360 — Times 10, move all digits 1 place value to the left

2 36 x 100 = 3 600 — Times 100, move all digits 2 place values to the left

3 36 x 1 000 = 36 000 — Times 1000, move all digits 3 place values to the left

To divide a whole number by a power of 10 you move all the digits a certain number of places to the right, as determined by the power. When you do this your number becomes smaller, for example...

1 36 ÷ 10 = 3.6 — Divide by 10, move all digits 1 place value to the right

2 36 ÷ 100 = 0.36 — Divide by 100, move all digits 2 place values to the right

3 36 ÷ 1 000 = 0.036 — Divide by 1000, move all digits 3 place values to the right

Integers 1

What are Integers?

Integers are all the whole numbers which are greater than zero, less than zero and zero itself. Above zero the numbers are positive although we don't write a **+** (plus) in front of them. Below zero the numbers are negative and these must have a **-** (minus) written in front of them. When you use positive and negative numbers, zero is the fixed point on the scale. All numbers relate to this point.

A number line, or scale, (which can be horizontal or vertical) can be a very useful aid for you to understand positive and negative numbers.

Positive and negative numbers are often used in everyday life e.g. to show temperatures above and below freezing or financial gain and loss.

A number line

A Bank Statement showing deposits and withdrawals.

LONSDALE BUILDING SOCIETY

Date	Description	Deposit	Withdrawal	Balance
11/12/03				£226.30
12/12/03	The Toy Shop		-£49.99	£176.31
13/12/03	Gas Bill		-£21.03	£155.28
14/12/03	Cheque	£25.00		£180.28
16/12/03	La Trattoria		-£32.98	£147.30
19/12/03	Rent		-£260.00	-£112.70

Ordering Integers

This means rearranging a series of positive and negative numbers in either ascending (lowest to highest) or descending (highest to lowest) order.

The simplest way is to collect together in two separate groups all the negative and positive numbers. If need be you can then use a number line to order the numbers.

Example

Rearrange the following temperatures in ascending order:
7°C, -1°C, 2°C, 5°C, -4°C, -2°C, 3°C, -8°C

Collect together in two separate groups (of negative and positive numbers) and order using a number line ...

...to give us the temperatures in ascending order: **-8°C, -4°C, -2°C, -1°C, 2°C, 3°C, 5°C, 7°C**

Integers 2

Addition & Subtraction of Integers

When you are adding or subtracting integers always draw a number line to help you. Positive numbers are counted to the right of the number line and negative numbers to the left.

Examples ...

1. At 6pm the temperature in Manchester was 6°C. By 10pm it had fallen by 8°C. The temperature at 10pm is therefore **6°C - 8°C**. On a number line this calculation can be shown by starting at 6 and then counting 8 to the left...

... 6°C - 8°C = -2°C

2. The temperature had fallen a further 6°C by 1am. On a number line this can be shown by starting at -2 and counting 6 places to the left...

... -2°C - 6°C = -8°C

Manchester 6°C

Multiplication & Division of Integers

When you are multiplying or dividing integers ignore any signs and multiply or divide the two numbers to get the number part of the answer. If the numbers have **like** signs the answer is **positive**, whereas if the numbers have **different** signs the answer is **negative**. This table shows all the possibilities:

Examples ...

1. 6 x -7 = -42
2. -12 x 8 = -96
3. -11 x -5 = 55
4. 75 ÷ -5 = -15
5. -200 ÷ 40 = -5
6. -99 ÷ -11 = 9

Order of Operations

Bidmas

The simplest possible calculation involves only one operation e.g. an addition or multiplication, which is easy enough to work out.

However, when a calculation involves more than one operation, you must carry them out in the order shown here.

BIDMAS

- **B** — BRACKETS
- **I** — INDICES (OR POWERS)
- **DM** — DIVISIONS AND MULTIPLICATIONS - THESE CAN BE DONE IN ANY ORDER
- **AS** — ADDITIONS AND SUBTRACTIONS - AGAIN IN ANY ORDER

Examples ...

1 $8 + 3 \times 4$
Do the multiplication first
$= 8 + 12$
Then the addition
$= 20$

2 $\dfrac{(14 + 6)}{4}$
Do the addition in the bracket first
$= \dfrac{20}{-4}$
Then the division
$= -5 \;(+ \div - = -)$

3 $4^2 - 2 \times 5$
Work out the square first
$= 16 - 2 \times 5$
Then the multiplication
$= 16 - 10$
Then the subtraction
$= 6$

Make sure that you do these examples again, only this time do the operations in the wrong order. You should get different answers which are wrong!

Use of Brackets

The insertion of a bracket (or brackets) into a calculation can drastically change the final answer.

Do remember that if you are asked to insert a bracket into a calculation that involves more than one operation there is always more than one possibility. Make sure that you try out all the different possibilities.

Example ...

Here is a calculation with no brackets in it.
$8 + 3 \times 4 - 2 = 8 + 12 - 2 = 20 - 2 = 18$
(or $8 + 10$)

If we now insert one bracket into the calculation the possible answers become...

$(8 + 3) \times 4 - 2 = 11 \times 4 - 2 = 44 - 2 = 42$

$8 + 3 \times (4 - 2) = 8 + 3 \times 2 = 8 + 6 = 14$

Rounding Numbers 1

Previously on page 4 we have rounded very large numbers to a given power of 10. We will now go a couple of stages further and round numbers to a given number of Decimal Places and Significant Figures.

Rounding a Number to 1 Decimal Place

These are numbers that are only allowed one digit after the decimal point. To round a number to 1 decimal place (1 d.p.) we must look at the **second** digit after the decimal point. There are two possibilities:

If the second digit after the decimal point is 4 **or less** (i.e. 0, 1, 2, 3 or 4) we leave the first digit after the decimal point as it is.

Examples ...

1. **7.43** to 1 d.p. is **7.4**.
2. **167.14** to 1 d.p. is **167.1**.

If the second digit after the decimal point is 5 **or more** (i.e. 5, 6, 7, 8 or 9) we **round up** and add 1 to the first digit after the decimal point.

Examples ...

1. **7.48** to 1 d.p. is **7.5**.
2. **53.7503** to 1 d.p. is **53.8**.

Rounding a Number to 2 or more Decimal Places

To round a number to 2 d.p. we are only allowed two digits after the decimal point. This time we must look at the **third** digit after the decimal point to decide whether we need to round up or to keep the second digit after the decimal point the same.

To round a number to 3 d.p. we must look at the **fourth** digit and so on. Unless a question tells you otherwise, always give money to 2 decimal places. Amounts of money are rounded to 2 d.p. in exactly the same way as below.

14.36482

= **14.3648** to 4 d.p. (stays same)

= **14.365** to 3 d.p. (round up)

= **14.36** to 2 d.p. (stays same)

= **14.4** to 1 d.p. (round up)

Rounding Numbers 2

Significant Figures for Numbers Greater Than 1

Rounding a number to a certain number of significant figures (s.f.) is very like rounding a number to a certain number of decimal places.

To round a number to 1 s.f. we need to look at the second digit and round up or leave the same. To round a number to 2 s.f. we need to look at the third digit and so on.

The number alongside is the attendance at a pop concert. It has 4 significant figures.

7000 to 1 s.f. (round up)

6800 to 2 s.f. (stays same)

6830 to 3 s.f. (round up)

Another Example ...

130.71 → to 4 s.f. is **130.7**
→ to 3 s.f. is **131**
→ to 2 s.f. is **130**
→ to 1 s.f. is **100**

NOTE:
130.71 has 5 significant figures. The 0 (zero) **does** count as it is in between digits.

Significant Figures for Numbers Less Than 1

These follow the same rules except we start counting our significant figures from the first digit greater than 0 (zero). For example ...

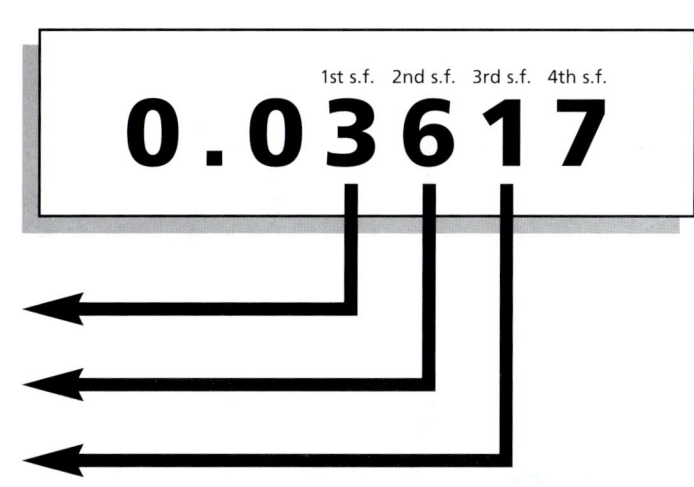

0.04 to 1 s.f. (round up)

0.036 to 2 s.f. (stays same)

0.0362 to 3 s.f. (round up)

Estimating & Checking

Estimating Answers

The answer to many calculations can be estimated by rounding off numbers within the calculations to 1 significant figure.

Examples ...

Estimate the answers to the following calculations:

1   71 + 18 - 26

$\cong$ 70 + 20 - 30

= 60 (Actual answer is 63)

2 $\dfrac{43 \times 2.9}{61.34}$

$\cong \dfrac{40 \times 3}{60}$

$= \dfrac{120}{60}$

= 2 (Actual answer is 2.03 (2 d.p.))

3 $\dfrac{3.6 \times 10.4}{7.7 - 3.1}$

$\cong \dfrac{4 \times 10}{8 - 3}$

$= \dfrac{40}{5}$

= 8 (Actual answer is 8.14 (2 d.p.))

4 $\dfrac{413 \times 4.87}{0.189}$

$\cong \dfrac{400 \times 5}{0.2}$

$= \dfrac{2000}{0.2}$

= 10 000

(Actual answer is 10 600 (3 d.p.))

Checking your Answers for Accuracy

Answers to calculations can be checked for accuracy by starting with your answer and working backwards, reversing the maths.

Examples ...

1   8 x 7 = 56 ⟶ $\dfrac{56}{8} = 7$ ✓ or $\dfrac{56}{7} = 8$ ✓

2

The table below shows the amount of money collected by a small local charity from October to December, using collecting tins at three different locations. Check it for accuracy.

MONTH	Location 1	Location 2	Location 3	TOTAL
Oct	28.08	16.73	18.23	63.04
Nov	32.96	21.01	18.16	72.13
Dec	26.12	19.57	16.03	61.72
TOTAL	87.16	57.31	52.42	**196.89**

For this example, there are several ways of checking it for accuracy. You could check the totals for each month (rows) or the totals for each location (columns). Finally, check the overall total.

- 63.04 + 72.13 + 61.72 = 196.89
  196.89 - 61.72 - 72.13 = 63.04 ✓

- 87.16 + 57.13 + 52.42 = 196.89
  196.89 - 52.42 - 57.31 = 87.16 ✓

Powers and Roots

Understanding Powers

Powers or indices show that a number is to be multiplied by itself a certain number of times.

4 x 4	= 4^2 (4 squared)
4 x 4 x 4	= 4^3 (4 cubed)
4 x 4 x 4 x 4	= 4^4 (4 to the power 4)
... and so on	

4^2 ← the power or index

Square Numbers

Numbers obtained by squaring a number are called square numbers, for example ...

4 squared = 4^2 = 4 x 4 = 16

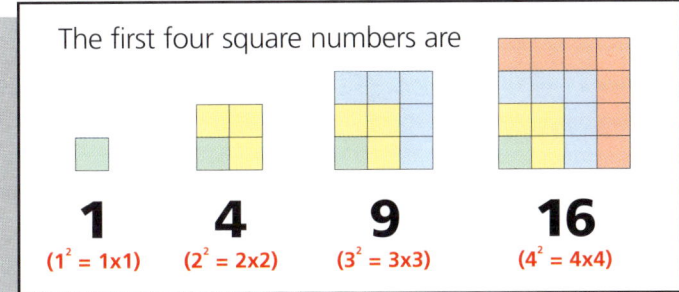

The first four square numbers are

1   4   9   16

(1^2 = 1x1)   (2^2 = 2x2)   (3^2 = 3x3)   (4^2 = 4x4)

Cube Numbers

Numbers obtained by cubing a number are called cube numbers, for example ...

4 cubed = 4^3 = 4 x 4 x 4 = 64

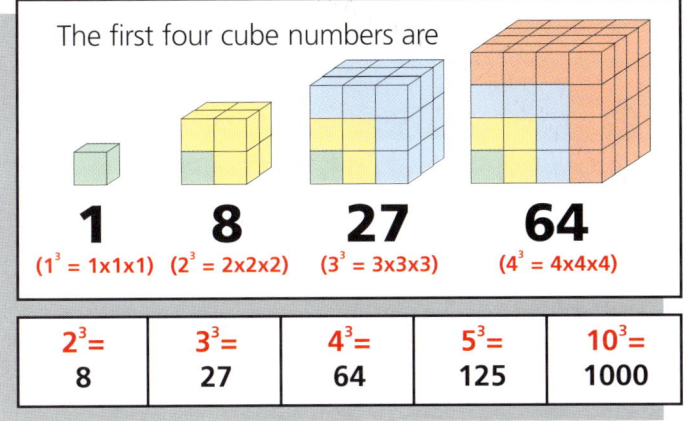

The first four cube numbers are

1   8   27   64

(1^3 = 1x1x1)   (2^3 = 2x2x2)   (3^3 = 3x3x3)   (4^3 = 4x4x4)

2^3= 8	3^3= 27	4^3= 64	5^3= 125	10^3= 1000

Example ...

Calculate the value of $2^2 \times 3^3$

$2^2 \times 3^3$ = (2 x 2) x (3 x 3 x 3) = 4 x 27 = 108

Powers of 10

Large numbers can often be written more easily by using a power of 10. For instance **3 x 10^6** is another way of writing **3 000 000**.

10^1 = 10	(ten)
10^2 = 100	(one hundred)
10^3 = 1 000	(one thousand)
10^4 = 10 000	(ten thousand)
10^5 = 100 000	(one hundred thousand)
10^6 = 1 000 000	(one million)

Square Roots

Since **5 x 5 = 25**, we call **5** the square root of **25**. i.e. that number which when multiplied by itself gives **25**. The symbol for a square root is $\sqrt{}$. Look at the following square roots:

$\sqrt{16}$ = 4 (because 4 x 4 = 16)
$\sqrt{9}$ = 3 (because 3 x 3 = 9)
$\sqrt{4}$ = 2 (because 2 x 2 = 4)

Remember though, not all square roots are whole numbers e.g. $\sqrt{10}$ = **3.162** approx.

2^2= 4	3^2= 9	4^2= 16	5^2= 25	6^2= 36	7^2= 49	8^2= 64
$\sqrt{4}$ = 2	$\sqrt{9}$ = 3	$\sqrt{16}$ = 4	$\sqrt{25}$ = 5	$\sqrt{36}$ = 6	$\sqrt{49}$ = 7	$\sqrt{64}$ = 8

9^2= 81	10^2= 100	11^2= 121	12^2= 144	13^2= 169	14^2= 196	15^2= 225
$\sqrt{81}$ = 9	$\sqrt{100}$ = 10	$\sqrt{121}$ = 11	$\sqrt{144}$ = 12	$\sqrt{169}$ = 13	$\sqrt{196}$ = 14	$\sqrt{225}$ = 15

Fractions 1

Understanding Simple Fractions

The diagram shows a whole pizza that has been cut into four equal parts (or slices). Each slice can be described as a fraction of the whole pizza and its value is $\frac{1}{4}$.

The pizza however could have been cut into any number of slices, where each slice is a different fraction of the whole pizza (see the diagrams below).

The top number of a fraction is called the **numerator** while the bottom number is called the **denominator**.

Equivalent Fractions

These are fractions that are equal. You can build chains of equivalent fractions by simply multiplying the numerator and denominator in the fraction by the same number.

1 This chain was formed using the two times table.

$$\frac{1}{4} \xrightarrow{\times 2} \frac{2}{8} \xrightarrow{\times 2} \frac{4}{16} \xrightarrow{\times 2} \frac{8}{32}$$

2 This chain was formed using the three times table.

$$\frac{1}{5} \xrightarrow{\times 3} \frac{3}{15} \xrightarrow{\times 3} \frac{9}{45} \xrightarrow{\times 3} \frac{27}{135}$$

Cancelling Fractions

You can also divide the numerator and denominator in a fraction by the same number to make them smaller. Chains of equivalent fractions that are cancelled down using division always come to an end when the fraction is expressed in its simplest form i.e. lowest terms.

1 $\frac{18}{27} \xrightarrow{\div 3} \frac{6}{9} \xrightarrow{\div 3} \frac{2}{3}$

2 $\frac{45}{60} \xrightarrow{\div 3} \frac{15}{20} \xrightarrow{\div 5} \frac{3}{4}$

3 $\frac{100}{140} \xrightarrow{\div 2} \frac{50}{70} \xrightarrow{\div 2} \frac{25}{35} \xrightarrow{\div 5} \frac{5}{7}$

Fractions 2

Ordering Fractions

To order fractions, write each fraction with a common denominator. If you are unsure choose the lowest number that is a multiple of all of the denominators given. You can then order the fractions by the 'size' of the numerators, for example ...

Arrange $\frac{9}{10}, \frac{4}{5}, \frac{7}{8}$ in ascending order.

Firstly write each fraction with a common denominator. The lowest number that is a multiple of 10, 5 and 8 is 40. Therefore ...

$$\frac{9}{10} \overset{\times 4}{\underset{\times 4}{=}} \frac{36}{40} \qquad \frac{4}{5} \overset{\times 8}{\underset{\times 8}{=}} \frac{32}{40} \qquad \frac{7}{8} \overset{\times 5}{\underset{\times 5}{=}} \frac{35}{40}$$

If we now compare the numerators we can arrange the fractions in ascending (lowest to highest) order.

In ascending order they are: $\frac{4}{5}, \frac{7}{8}, \frac{9}{10}$

Also when you have fractions with common denominators it is possible to find other fractions that lie between these fractions.

For example, from above $\frac{4}{5} = \frac{32}{40}$ and $\frac{7}{8} = \frac{35}{40}$. It should be obvious that we can write two other fractions with denominator 40 which are greater than $\frac{4}{5}$ but less than $\frac{7}{8}$. They would be $\frac{33}{40}$ and $\frac{34}{40}$, which cancels down to $\frac{17}{20}$.

Improper Fractions and Mixed Numbers

Some fractions are known as improper because they are 'top heavy' i.e. the top number is bigger than the bottom number. $\frac{5}{4}$ is 'top heavy'. It needs simplifying into a mixed number so that it is easier to read and understand.

If we go back to our pizza on the previous page, then $\frac{5}{4}$ would be one whole pizza cut into four slices, plus one extra slice from another pizza.

In other words ...

$$\frac{5}{4} = \frac{4}{4} + \frac{1}{4} = 1\frac{1}{4}$$

Other Examples ...

① $\frac{13}{5} = \frac{5}{5} + \frac{5}{5} + \frac{3}{5} = 2\frac{3}{5}$

② $\frac{19}{6} = \frac{6}{6} + \frac{6}{6} + \frac{6}{6} + \frac{1}{6} = 3\frac{1}{6}$

$19 \div 6 = 3 + \frac{1}{6}$ left over!

The examples above show improper fractions being changed into mixed numbers. The reverse process can also be used to change mixed numbers into improper fractions.

Fractions 3

Addition of Fractions

Two fractions can be added very easily providing they have common denominators.

$$\frac{2}{5} = \frac{8}{20} \quad \frac{2}{5} + \frac{3}{4} \quad \frac{3}{4} = \frac{15}{20}$$
$$= \frac{8}{20} + \frac{15}{20}$$
$$= \frac{23}{20}$$
$$= 1\frac{3}{20}$$

With mixed numbers, add the whole numbers and fractions separately and then combine.

$$2\frac{2}{3} + 3\frac{1}{7}$$
$$= (2 + 3) + \left(\frac{2}{3} + \frac{1}{7}\right)$$
$$= 5 + \left(\frac{14}{21} + \frac{3}{21}\right)$$
$$= 5 + \frac{17}{21} = 5\frac{17}{21}$$

Subtraction of Fractions

As for addition, two fractions can be subtracted very easily providing they have common denominators.

$$\frac{7}{8} = \frac{21}{24} \quad \frac{7}{8} - \frac{2}{3} \quad \frac{2}{3} = \frac{16}{24}$$
$$= \frac{21}{24} - \frac{16}{24}$$
$$= \frac{5}{24}$$

With mixed numbers, subtract the whole numbers and fractions separately and then combine.

$$4\frac{1}{2} - 1\frac{2}{5}$$
$$= (4 - 1) + \left(\frac{1}{2} - \frac{2}{5}\right)$$
$$= 3 + \left(\frac{5}{10} - \frac{4}{10}\right)$$
$$= 3 + \left(\frac{1}{10}\right)$$
$$= 3\frac{1}{10}$$

Multiplication and Division of Fractions

Multiplying an integer by a fraction, such as $1 \times \frac{1}{5}$ can be thought of as dividing by **5**. When the fraction is $\frac{4}{5}$ we can think of $1 \times \frac{4}{5}$ as a multiplication by **4** followed by a division by **5**.

To multiply two fractions all you have to do is multiply together the two numerators and the two denominators.

$$\frac{2}{3} \times \frac{4}{5} = \frac{2 \times 4}{3 \times 5} = \frac{8}{15}$$

Division of two fractions is the same as multiplication, except that you turn the second fraction (that is doing the dividing) upside down and change the division sign to a multiplication sign.

$$\frac{2}{3} \div \frac{4}{5} = \frac{2}{3} \times \frac{5}{4} = \frac{2 \times 5}{3 \times 4} = \frac{10}{12} = \frac{5}{6}$$

To multiply or divide a fraction by an integer, change the integer to an improper fraction. For example, **4** as an improper fraction is $\frac{4}{1}$. You can then do the multiplication or division as normal.

$$\frac{4}{7} \times 3 = \frac{4}{7} \times \frac{3}{1} = \frac{4 \times 3}{7 \times 1} = \frac{12}{7} = 1\frac{5}{7}$$

$$\frac{2}{3} \div 10 = \frac{2}{3} \div \frac{10}{1} = \frac{2}{3} \times \frac{1}{10} = \frac{2 \times 1}{3 \times 10} = \frac{2}{30} = \frac{1}{15}$$

Calculations Involving Fractions

Calculating a Fraction of a Quantity

To find a fraction of any quantity all you have to do is multiply the fraction by the quantity. In other words 'of' means 'times' or 'multiply' (×).

Examples...

① Calculate $\frac{4}{5}$ of 60kg.

$\frac{4}{5}$ of 60kg = $\frac{4}{5}$ × 60 ('of' means '×')

$= \frac{4}{5} \times \frac{60}{1}$

$= \frac{240}{5}$

$= 48$kg

② A brand new car costing £9 000 will lose $\frac{1}{5}$ of its value in the first year. What is the value of the car after the first year?

Before we can calculate its value we need to calculate the loss.

Loss = $\frac{1}{5}$ of £9 000 = $\frac{1}{5}$ × 9 000 = $\frac{1}{5} \times \frac{9\,000}{1} = \frac{9\,000}{5}$ = £1 800 ('of' means '×')

Value of car after the first year = £9 000 - £1 800 = £7 200.

Expressing One Quantity as a Fraction of Another Quantity

Firstly you must make sure that both quantities are in the same units. Then, to express the relationship as a fraction, the first quantity becomes the numerator (top number) and the second quantity becomes the denominator (bottom number). If need be, write the fraction in its lowest terms.

Examples...

① Write 30 out of 120 as a fraction.

30 out of 120 = $\frac{30}{120} = \frac{1}{4}$

② Express 36 seconds as a fraction of 2 minutes. Both quantities must be in the same units, so change 2 minutes into seconds.

2 minutes = 2 × 60s = 120s, so ...

36s as a fraction of 120s = $\frac{36}{120} = \frac{3}{10}$

Decimals 1

Understanding Simple Decimals

When you use money and metric measures, such as millimetres, litres or grams, you often use simple decimals. Decimals are an easy kind of fraction - easy because the ten 'times' table is the only one ever needed! If you think of a pizza, with decimals the whole pizza is only ever divided into ten, a hundred or a thousand pieces.

where each slice = $\frac{1}{10}$ or **0.1**

0.1   0.2   0.3   0.4   0.5   etc.

Place Value in Decimal Numbers

We've already seen that all the digits in a whole number have a place value. In a decimal number, all digits to the right of the decimal point also have a place value.

Decimal Number	Place Value of Digits					
	10 (Tens)	1 (Units)	. (DECIMAL POINT)	$\frac{1}{10}$ (Tenths)	$\frac{1}{100}$ (Hundredths)	$\frac{1}{1000}$ (Thousandths)
0.06		0		0	6	
0.507		0		5	0	7
1.39		1		3	9	
74.258	7	4		2	5	8

The position of the decimal point is just as important as the digits themselves. Misplacing the decimal point makes a huge difference because all the place values change. For example, in a long jump contest a pupil records a jump of 4.37m. Imagine the excitement if the distance was recorded as 43.7m!

Decimals and Money

An amount of money is often written as a decimal, where the decimal point separates the amount in pounds from the amount in pence. Remember, any amount of money involving pounds and pence is always written to 2 decimal places (2d.p.), for example...

- Six pounds forty seven pence is written as **£6.47**

- Twelve pounds one pence is written as **£12.01 and not £12.1**

- £5 can be written as **£5.00**

- 47p can be written as **£0.47**

Decimals 2

Recurring and Terminating Decimals

Some fractions don't convert very conveniently into decimals because they just go on and on and on …

$\frac{1}{3}$ as a decimal is 0.33333333 etc.

$\frac{3}{11}$ as a decimal is 0.27272727 etc.

These are called **recurring** decimals to distinguish them from **terminating** decimals.

e.g. $0.7 = \frac{7}{10}$ $0.25 = \frac{25}{100}$ or $\frac{1}{4}$ $0.35 = \frac{35}{100}$ or $\frac{7}{20}$

Ordering Decimals

This means rearranging a series of decimals in either ascending (lowest to highest) or descending (highest to lowest) order. A useful method is to line up all the decimal points of the numbers in a vertical line. Then you can start with the first column on the left, and work along each column of numbers (left to right) to decide which is the biggest number.

Example …

Rearrange the following in ascending order:
0.54, 5.4, 0.45, 4.5

Line up the decimal points.

0.54	0.45
5.4	0.54
0.45	4.5
4.5	5.4

Addition and Subtraction of Decimals

As for whole numbers the place values of the digits must line up one on top of the other, although an easy way is to simply line up your decimal points. Do remember to bring the decimal point down to your answer.

Examples …

```
   343.62          63.184
 + 17.59         -  5.091
   ------          ------
   361.21          58.093
```

Multiplication of Decimals

Multiplication of Decimal Numbers by Powers of 10

To multiply a decimal number by a power of 10 e.g. 10 (10^1), 100 (10^2), 1000 (10^3), all you have to do is move all the digits a certain number of place values to the left. When you do this your number becomes bigger. For example ...

1) 9.3 x 10 = 93

Digits move one place value to the left and the number becomes 10 times bigger.

2) 0.47 x 100 = 47

Digits move two place values to the left and the number becomes 100 times bigger.

3) 13.27 x 1 000 = 13 270

Digits move three place values to the left and the number becomes 1000 times bigger.

Multiplication of Positive Numbers by Decimal Numbers between 0 and 1

If you multiply any positive number by a decimal number between 0 and 1 the answer is always smaller than the positive number you started with, for example ...

1) 10 x 0.5 = 5

2) 5 x 0.3 = 1.5

3) 986 x 0.01 = 9.86

Multiplication of Decimal Numbers by Whole and Decimal Numbers

All you do is ignore the decimal points and multiply as you would whole numbers. You put the decimal point in at the end. In your answer, the number of digits after the decimal point should be the same as the total number of digits after the decimal points in the numbers being multiplied. For example ...

1) 2.73 x 18

Multiply as you would whole numbers (see page 6)

```
    2 7 3
x      1 8
---------
  2 7 3 0
  2 1 8 4
---------
  4 9 1 4
```

Then, count digits after decimal point in numbers being multiplied and transfer to answer.

2.73 x 18 = 49.14

Therefore **2.73 x 18 = 49.14**

2) 17.5 x 9.6

Multiply as you would whole numbers.

```
    1 7 5
x      9 6
---------
  1 5 7 5 0
  1 0 5 0
---------
  1 6 8 0 0
```

Then, count digits after decimal point in numbers being multiplied and transfer to answer.

17.5 x 9.6 = 16800

Therefore **17.5 x 9.6 = 168.00**

Division of Decimals

Division of Decimal Numbers by Powers of 10

The process is the reverse of multiplying decimal numbers by powers of 10. With division all the digits move a certain number of place values to the right. When you do this your number becomes smaller. For example ...

① **46.3 ÷ 10 = 4.63**

   Digits move one place value to the right and the number becomes 10 times smaller.

② **3.61 ÷ 100 = 0.0361**

   Digits move two place values to the right and the number becomes 100 times smaller.

③ **473.2 ÷ 1000 = 0.4732**

   Digits move three place values to the right and the number becomes 1000 times smaller.

Division of Positive Numbers by Decimal Numbers between 0 and 1

If you divide any positive number by a decimal number between 0 and 1 the answer is always bigger than the positive number you started with, for example ...

① **10 ÷ 0.5 = 20**

② **5 ÷ 0.4 = 12.5**

③ **471 ÷ 0.01 = 47 100**

Division of Decimal Numbers by Whole Numbers and Decimal Numbers

Division of a decimal number by a whole number is the same as the division of whole numbers (see page 6). The only exception is that you must remember to take the decimal point up to your answer.

13.2 ÷ 6

Divide as you would whole numbers

```
      2.2
6 ) 13.2
    12
     1 2
     1 2
       0
```

Remember to take the decimal point up to the answer

Therefore **13.2 ÷ 6 = 2.2**

Division of a decimal number by another decimal number is slightly more tricky. Before you start, multiply both numbers by 10, 100 etc. until the number doing the dividing is a whole number. The process from now on is the same as the example above.

1.92 ÷ 1.2

Multiply both numbers by 10 to make the number doing the dividing a whole number.
1.92 x 10 = 19.2, 1.2 x 10 = 12
Divide as you would whole numbers.

```
       1.6
12 ) 19.2
     12
      7 2
      7 2
        0
```

Remember to take the decimal point up to the answer

Therefore **1.92 ÷ 1.2 = 1.6**

Percentages 1

Understanding Simple Percentages

Percentages are used in everyday life, from pay rises to price reductions. This helps us to make easy comparisons. When you understand the basics of percentages they are even easier than decimals or fractions. They focus on the whole being equal to one hundred i.e. the whole is one hundred per cent. So, if someone gives you 50% of a whole pizza this tells you the 'number of parts per 100' you have e.g. 50% is 50 parts per 100 or $\frac{50}{100}$

10% **20%** **30%** **40%** **50%** **etc.**

Calculating a Percentage of a Quantity

Examples...

1 Calculate 40% of 50cm.

40% means 40 parts per 100 or $\frac{40}{100}$ and 'of' means 'times' or 'multiply'(x).

40% of 50cm = $\frac{40}{100}$ x 50 = $\frac{40 \times 50}{100}$

= 20cm

2 Calculate 15% of £4.80. Give your answer in pence.

£4.80 = 4.80 x 100p = 480p

15% means 15 parts out of 100 or $\frac{15}{100}$ and 'of' means 'times' (x).

15% of 480p = $\frac{15}{100}$ x 480

= $\frac{15 \times 480}{100}$

= 72p

Expressing One Quantity as a Percentage of Another Quantity

Make sure that both quantities are in the same units. Firstly express one quantity as a fraction of the other, where the first quantity becomes the numerator (top number) and the second quantity becomes the denominator (bottom number). All you have to do then is multiply this fraction by 100%.

Examples...

1 Write 18 out of 30 as a percentage.

18 out of 30 = $\frac{18}{30}$ x 100%

= $\frac{18 \times 100}{30}$ = 60%

2 Express 30cm as a percentage of 3m. Both quantities must be in the same units, so change 3m into centimetres.
3m = 3 x 100cm = 300cm, so ...

30cm as a % of 300cm = $\frac{30}{300}$ x 100%

= $\frac{30 \times 100}{300}$ = 10%

Percentages 2

Examples ...

1 A standard box of breakfast cereal weighs 500g. Special boxes contain an extra 25%. Calculate the weight of a special box of cereal.

Firstly calculate the extra increase in weight ...

25% of 500g = $\frac{25}{100}$ × 500g = $\frac{25 \times 500}{100}$ = 125g

... then add it to the weight of a standard box of cereal.

Weight of special box = 500g + 125g = 625g.

An alternative method would be as follows: A standard box of cereal is to be increased by 25%. If a standard box is 100%, a special box will be 100% + 25% = 125%.

125% = $\frac{125}{100}$ = 1.25

In other words, the weight of a special box is 1.25 times the weight of a standard box.

Weight of special box = 1.25 × 500g = 625g.

---

2 On 1st January 2002 John buys a house for £100 000. If house price inflation then runs at 15% per annum for the next two years, how much will his house be worth ...
a) on December 31st 2002?
b) on December 31st 2003?

a) Original cost = £100 000

£100 000 × $\frac{115}{100}$

= £115 000

$\frac{115}{100}$ represents a 15% increase

b) Cost after 1 year = £115 000

£115 000 × $\frac{115}{100}$

= £132 250

$\frac{115}{100}$ represents a 15% increase

3 James buys a Volkswagen Golf brand new for £10 000. Unfortunately it depreciates by 18% in the first year and by 15% in the second. How much would it then be worth?

First year:

£10 000 × $\frac{82}{100}$

= £8 200

$\frac{82}{100}$ represents an 18% decrease

Second year:

£8 200 × $\frac{85}{100}$

= £6 970

$\frac{85}{100}$ represents a 15% decrease

Percentages 3

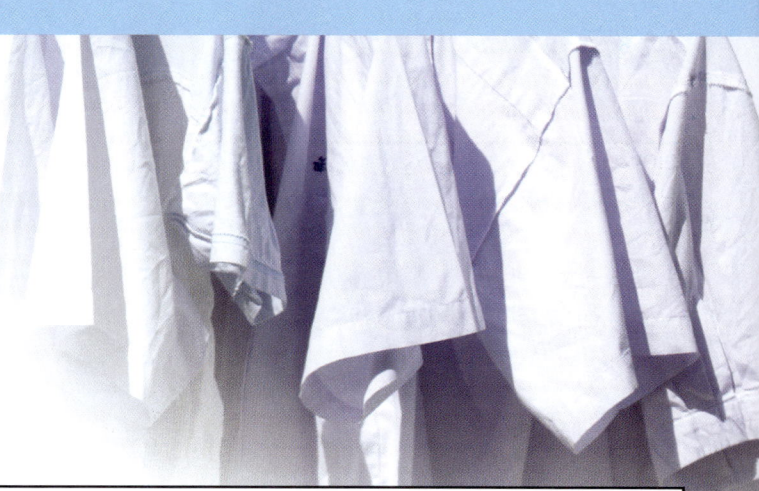

Calculations Involving Comparisons

These are calculations where the original amount has been increased or decreased by a certain percentage to a transformed amount. You must remember that the original amount is always equal to 100% and that the transformed amount will always be a percentage that is above or below 100%.

Examples ...

1 A shop offers 10% off all its clothes. A shirt has a sale price of £27. What was the original price of the shirt?

Original price of shirt = 100%
Sale price of shirt = 100% - 10%
= 90%

There has been a decrease of 10%

∴ 90% = £27   (÷90)
   1% = £0.30   (÷90)
∴ 100% = £30   (×100)   (×100)

So the original price of the shirt was £30

---

2 In 2004 a company allocated £15 000 of its budget to be spent on advertising. This was a 20% increase on the money spent on advertising in 2003. How much money did the company spend on advertising in 2003?

Original amount in this question is the money spent on advertising in 2003.

Money spent on advertising in 2003 = 100%
Money spent on advertising in 2004 = 100% + 20%
There has been an increase of 20% = **120%**

∴ 120% = £15 000   (÷120)
    1% = £125   (÷120)
∴ 100% = £12 500   (×100)   (×100)

So the advertising budget for 2003 was £12 500

2003

2004

Converting Between Systems

Below is a summary of how to convert between fractions, decimals and percentages. You may start at any of the three points. Trace around the charts and see how you can move from one system to another by following simple rules.

Divide the numerator (top number) by the denominator (bottom number)

$$\frac{1}{4} = 0.25$$

$25\% = \frac{25}{100} = \frac{1}{4}$
Put your % as a fraction over 100 and cancel down

$0.25 = 0.25 \times 100\% = 25\%$
Multiply by 100

FRACTION $\frac{1}{4}$ ← **PERCENTAGE** 25% ← **DECIMAL** 0.25

Multiply by 100
$\frac{1}{4} = \frac{1}{4} \times 100\% = 25\%$

Divide by 100
$25\% = \frac{25}{100} = 0.25$

$$0.25 = \frac{0.25}{1} \overset{\times 10}{=} \frac{2.5}{10} \overset{\times 10}{=} \frac{25}{100} = \frac{1}{4}$$

Divide by 1 and then multiply numerator and denominator by 10's until the numerator becomes a whole number. Finally, cancel down if need be.

Other Examples...

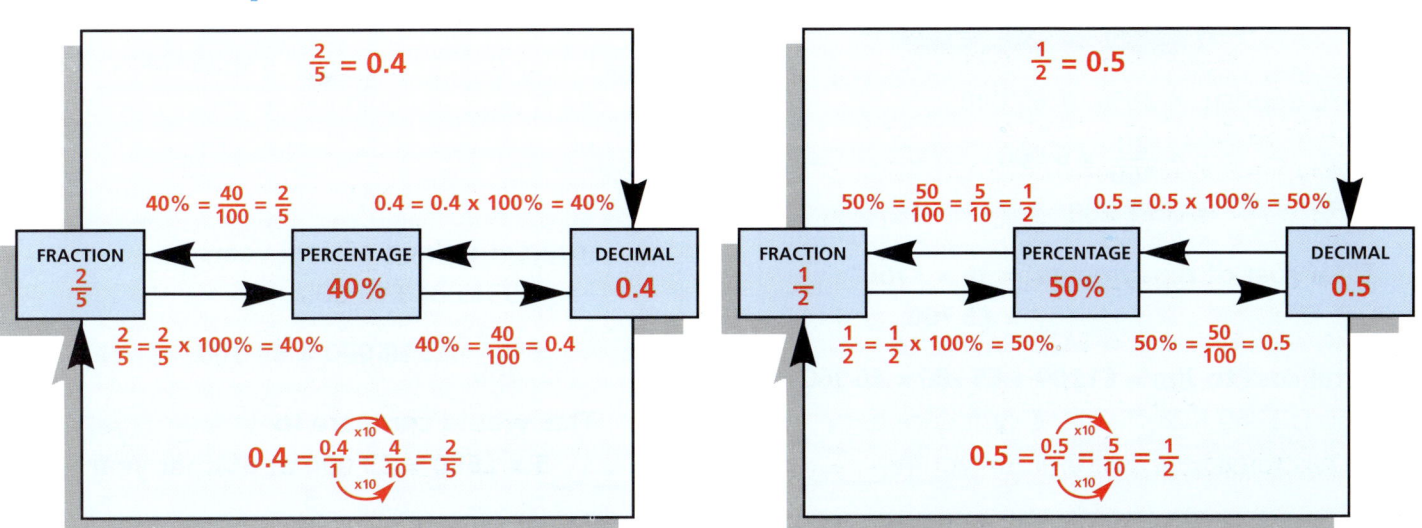

Everyday Maths 1

VAT

Value Added Tax or VAT is charged on goods you buy or any services you receive. Penny wants to buy this radio cassette player. How much will it cost her if VAT is charged at a rate of $17\frac{1}{2}\%$?

$$\begin{aligned} \text{VAT} &= 17\tfrac{1}{2}\% \text{ of } £50 \\ &= \frac{17\tfrac{1}{2}}{100} \times £50 \\ &= £8.75 \end{aligned}$$

Therefore total cost
$$\begin{aligned} &= £50 + £8.75 \\ &= £58.75 \end{aligned}$$

Purchasing on Credit

This is when you pay a deposit on a purchase and then you make a number of repayments spread over a certain period of time.

Example …

Jim is buying a car on credit. How much will it cost him altogether?

£6,000 or 20% Deposit & 36 monthly repayments of £160

$$\begin{aligned} 20\% \text{ deposit} &= 20\% \text{ of } £6\,000 \\ &= \frac{20}{100} \times 6\,000 \\ &= £1\,200 \end{aligned}$$

Total cost of repayments $= 36 \times £160$
$ = £5\,760$

Total cost to Jim $= £1\,200 + £5\,760 = £6\,960$
(This is £960 more than the cash price but he has spread the cost over 36 months)

Simple Interest

1 Mr and Mrs Smith have just won £10 000 on the lottery. They decide that they want to invest this money for 2 years. Mr Smith wants to invest the money at 6% simple interest. How much interest will he gain after 2 years?

Interest gained after 1st year
$= 6\% \text{ of } £10\,000$
$= \frac{6}{100} \times £10\,000 = £600$

> With simple interest the interest gained (£600) is not added to the amount invested so it does not earn interest in the next year

Interest gained after 2nd year
$= £600$ (same as 1st year)

Total interest gained
$= £600 + £600 = £1\,200$

2 If they put the money in a special account for 5 years it would pay terminal interest of 33%. Would this be better than 6% per year for 5 years?

Interest gained after 5 years
$= 33\% \text{ of } £10\,000$
$= \frac{33}{100} \times £10\,000 = £3\,300$

This would compare to
$5 \times £600 = £3\,000$ at 6% per year

Everyday Maths 2

Household Bills

More times than not these are worked out using 'common sense'. Here is a home-owner's electricity bill for one quarter.

The number of units used is found by subtracting the two meter readings

786 units x 7.5 pence per unit = £58.95

You have to pay this regardless of how much electricity you use

5% of £69.40 = $\frac{5}{100}$ x £69.40 = £3.47

£69.40 + £3.47 = £72.87

Understanding Tables and Charts

The secret to understanding tables and charts is to identify the relevant data. Once you've done this all you need to use is a bit of 'common sense'.

Example ...

A rail company operating trains out of Petersfield decides to offer cheap 'Off Peak' fares on services that arrive at London Waterloo after 10am. If a customer who usually catches the 0833 service from Petersfield decides to wait for the first Off Peak train, to take advantage of the offer, what will be the difference in his journey time?

The first thing to do is to identify the relevant data. This is in the third and fourth columns of the timetable shown opposite and has been highlighted for this purpose.

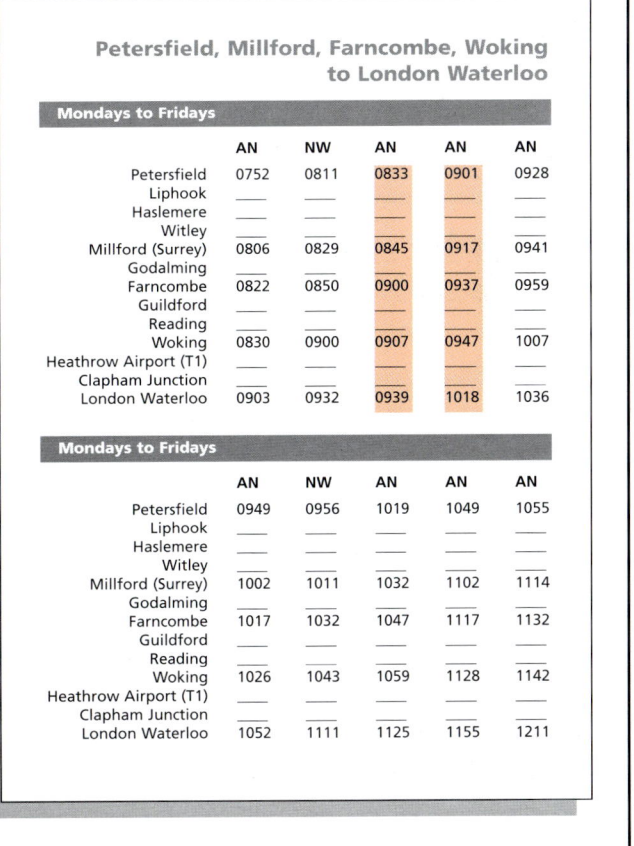

Usual journey time = Arrival Time - Departure Time
= 0939hrs - 0833hrs
= 1hr 6min

Remember to calculate hours & minutes separately

Off Peak journey time = Arrival Time - Departure Time
= 1018hrs - 0901hrs
= 1hr 17min

Difference in time = 1hr 17min - 1hr 6min
= 11min

Ratio and Proportion 1

What is a Ratio?

A ratio is a comparison between two or more quantities. Here we have two columns of coins. The first column has ten £1 coins and the second column has six 2p coins. To compare the two sets of coins we can say that the ratio of the number of £1 coins to 2p coins is **10 to 6 or 10 : 6**

This is like saying $\frac{10}{16}$ are £1 coins while $\frac{6}{16}$ are 2p coins. Ratios can be simplified into their simplest form, just like fractions ...

$$\div 2 \left(\begin{array}{c} 10 : 6 \\ = 5 : 3 \end{array} \right) \div 2$$

A ratio of **5 : 3** means that for every five £1 coins there are three 2p coins. The above ratio can also be written in the form **1 : n** by dividing both numbers in the ratio by 5 ...

$$\div 5 \left(\begin{array}{c} 5 : 3 \\ = 1 : 0.6 \end{array} \right) \div 5$$

It could be written in the form **n : 1** by dividing both numbers in the ratio by 3 ...

$$\div 3 \left(\begin{array}{c} 5 : 3 \\ = 1.6 : 1 \end{array} \right) \div 3$$

Example

A bag of carrots weighs 300g and a bag of potatoes 1.5kg. Calculate the ratio of weight of carrots to weight of potatoes.

Both quantities must be in the same units so, **1.5kg = 1.5 x 1 000g = 1 500g**

Ratio of weight of carrots to weight of potatoes is ...

$$\div 300 \left(\begin{array}{c} 300g : 1\,500g \\ = 1 : 5 \end{array} \right) \div 300$$

Ratios and Fractions

A ratio can be written as a fraction and vice versa.

Example

If $\frac{2}{5}$ of a class are boys what is the ratio of boys to girls? Give your answer in the form 1 : n.

The ratio of boys to girls is therefore...

$$\times 5 \left(\begin{array}{c} \frac{2}{5} : \frac{3}{5} \\ = 2 : 3 \end{array} \right) \times 5$$

Written in the form **1 : n** it is...

$$\div 2 \left(\begin{array}{c} 2 : 3 \\ = 1 : 1.5 \end{array} \right) \div 2$$

In other words for any one boy in the class there are one and a half girls!

Ratio and Proportion 2

Dividing a Quantity in a Given Ratio

Examples ...

£60 is to be divided between Jon and Pat in the ratio 2 : 3. How much money does each one receive?

> We need to divide £60 in the ratio 2 : 3

The digits in the ratio are called parts. Jon gets 2 parts and Pat gets 3 parts. The total number of parts is **2 + 3 = 5 parts** which is equal to £60. Therefore ...

÷5 (5 parts = £60) ÷5
    1 part = £12

Since we now know the 'value' of 1 part we can work out how much money Jon and Pat get.

Jon gets 2 parts = 2 x £12 = £24
Pat gets 3 parts = 3 x £12 = £36

> Check: £24 + £36 = £60

❷ Three brothers aged 6, 9 and 15 decide grudgingly to share a tin of toffees in the ratio of their ages. If the tin contains 240 toffees how many toffees does each brother get?

> We need to divide 240 toffees in the ratio 6 : 9 : 15

> Whenever possible cancel down your ratio to make things simpler

÷3 (6 : 9 : 15) ÷3
    = 2 : 3 : 5

Total number of parts
= 2 + 3 + 5 = 10 parts

Therefore ...

÷10 (10 parts = 240 toffees) ÷10
     1 part = 24 toffees

Brother aged 6 gets 2 x 24 = 48 toffees
Brother aged 9 gets 3 x 24 = 72 toffees
Brother aged 15 gets 5 x 24 = 120 toffees

> Check: 48 + 72 + 120 = 240 toffees

Increasing and Decreasing a Quantity in Direct Proportion

Example ...

A recipe to make 10 flapjack cakes requires, among other ingredients, 180g of butter. How much butter does a cook need to use if she wants to make
a) 6 flapjack cakes?
b) 25 flapjack cakes?

This is an example of a quantity (e.g. butter) that increases or decreases in direct proportion to the amount of cakes needed. The more cakes that are needed the greater the amount of butter needed and vice versa.

> The easiest way is to work out the amount of butter needed to make 1 flapjack cake.

÷10 (10 cakes require 180g of butter) ÷10
     1 cake requires 18g of butter

a) **6 flapjack cakes require**
   6 x 18g = 108g of butter

b) **25 flapjack cakes require**
   25 x 18g = 450g of butter

The Basics of Algebra

Algebra is a branch of mathematics where letters and other symbols are used to represent numbers and quantities in expressions, equations, identities and formulae. Algebra follows the same rules as arithmetic.

Algebraic Expressions

An algebraic expression is a collection of connected letters, numbers and arithmetical symbols. Here are some simple expressions and their meanings.

Algebraic Expression	What it means
$2a$	$a + a$ or $2 \times a$
ab	$a \times b$ (or $b \times a$)
$\frac{a}{b}$	$a \div b$
$3a - b$	$(3 \times a) - b$
c^2	$c \times c$
$4mn$	$4 \times m \times n$
x^2	$x \times x$
a^3	$a \times a \times a$
$4x^2y$	$4 \times x \times x \times y$
$(4a)^2$	$4a \times 4a$

Collecting Like Terms

Many expressions can be simplified by collecting together like terms.

Examples ...

1 $a + 2a$ is more simply $3a$

2 $5x - 8x + 7x$ is more simply $4x$

When your expression contains 'different' like terms, rearrange and collect together all like terms before you simplify.

3 $6b + 3c - 4b$
= $\underline{6b - 4b} + 3c$
    Like terms
= $2b + 3c$

4 $-4x + 3 + 7x - 8$
= $\underline{-4x + 7x} + \underline{3 - 8}$
    Like terms   Like terms
= $3x - 5$

5 $4x + 7y - x - 3y$
= $\underline{4x - x} + \underline{7y - 3y}$
    Like terms   Like terms
= $3x + 4y$

6 $5pq - 7rs + 8qp + 2sr$
= $\underline{5pq + 8pq} - \underline{7rs + 2rs}$
   Like terms   Like terms
   since 'pq' is the   since 'rs' is the
   same as 'qp'   same as 'sr'
= $13pq - 5rs$.

Identities

$a + a + a = 3a$ and $a + 2a = 3a$ are both examples of identities and not equations since $3a$ is simply a different way of expressing the two examples. In other words, what we have on the left-hand side of the equal sign is no different to what we have on the right-hand side of the equal sign. $5x - 8x + 7x = 4x$ is another example of an identity.

Ratio and Proportion 2

Dividing a Quantity in a Given Ratio

Examples ...

£60 is to be divided between Jon and Pat in the ratio 2 : 3. How much money does each one receive?

> We need to divide £60 in the ratio 2 : 3

The digits in the ratio are called parts. Jon gets 2 parts and Pat gets 3 parts. The total number of parts is **2 + 3 = 5 parts** which is equal to £60. Therefore ...

÷5 (5 parts = £60) ÷5
    1 part = £12

Since we now know the 'value' of 1 part we can work out how much money Jon and Pat get.

Jon gets 2 parts = 2 x £12 = £24
Pat gets 3 parts = 3 x £12 = £36

> Check: £24 + £36 = £60

② Three brothers aged 6, 9 and 15 decide grudgingly to share a tin of toffees in the ratio of their ages. If the tin contains 240 toffees how many toffees does each brother get?

> We need to divide 240 toffees in the ratio 6 : 9 : 15

> Whenever possible cancel down your ratio to make things simpler

÷3 (6 : 9 : 15) ÷3
    = 2 : 3 : 5

Total number of parts
= 2 + 3 + 5 = 10 parts

Therefore ...

÷10 (10 parts = 240 toffees) ÷10
     1 part = 24 toffees

Brother aged 6 gets 2 x 24 = 48 toffees
Brother aged 9 gets 3 x 24 = 72 toffees
Brother aged 15 gets 5 x 24 = 120 toffees

> Check: 48 + 72 + 120 = 240 toffees

Increasing and Decreasing a Quantity in Direct Proportion

Example ...

A recipe to make 10 flapjack cakes requires, among other ingredients, 180g of butter. How much butter does a cook need to use if she wants to make
a) 6 flapjack cakes?
b) 25 flapjack cakes?

This is an example of a quantity (e.g. butter) that increases or decreases in direct proportion to the amount of cakes needed. The more cakes that are needed the greater the amount of butter needed and vice versa.

> The easiest way is to work out the amount of butter needed to make 1 flapjack cake.

÷10 (10 cakes require 180g of butter) ÷10
     1 cake requires 18g of butter

a) 6 flapjack cakes require
   6 x 18g = 108g of butter

b) 25 flapjack cakes require
   25 x 18g = 450g of butter

The Basics of Algebra

Algebra is a branch of mathematics where letters and other symbols are used to represent numbers and quantities in expressions, equations, identities and formulae. Algebra follows the same rules as arithmetic.

Algebraic Expressions

An algebraic expression is a collection of connected letters, numbers and arithmetical symbols. Here are some simple expressions and their meanings.

Algebraic Expression	What it means
2a	a + a or 2 x a
ab	a x b (or b x a)
$\frac{a}{b}$	a ÷ b
3a - b	(3 x a) - b
c^2	c x c
4mn	4 x m x n
x^2	x x x
a^3	a x a x a
$4x^2y$	4 x x x x x y
$(4a)^2$	4a x 4a

Collecting Like Terms

Many expressions can be simplified by collecting together like terms.

Examples ...

1. **a + 2a** is more simply **3a**
2. **5x - 8x + 7x** is more simply **4x**

When your expression contains 'different' like terms, rearrange and collect together all like terms before you simplify.

3.   6b + 3c - 4b
   = 6b - 4b + 3c
        Like terms
   = 2b + 3c

4.   - 4x + 3 + 7x - 8
   = - 4x + 7x + 3 - 8
       Like terms Like terms
   = 3x - 5

5.   4x + 7y - x - 3y
   = 4x - x + 7y - 3y
      Like terms Like terms
   = 3x + 4y

6.   5pq - 7rs + 8qp + 2sr
   = 5pq + 8pq - 7rs + 2rs
      Like terms   Like terms
      since 'pq' is the since 'rs' is the
      same as 'qp'   same as 'sr'
   = 13pq - 5rs.

Identities

a + a + a = 3a and **a + 2a = 3a** are both examples of identities and not equations since **3a** is simply a different way of expressing the two examples. In other words, what we have on the left-hand side of the equal sign is no different to what we have on the right-hand side of the equal sign. **5x - 8x + 7x = 4x** is another example of an identity.

Substitution

This involves substituting numbers for letters in expressions. The simplest substitution would involve only one operation (i.e. an addition, multiplication etc.). However, when a substitution involves more than one operation, you must make them in the order shown below.

Also, since you are expected to be able to substitute positive and negative numbers into expressions turn back to page 8 to refresh yourself on the multiplication and division of integers.

BIDMAS

- **B** — BRACKETS
- **I** — INDICES
- **DM** — DIVISIONS AND MULTIPLICATIONS - THESE CAN BE DONE IN ANY ORDER
- **AS** — ADDITIONS AND SUBTRACTIONS - AGAIN IN ANY ORDER

Examples ...

If **a = 3, b = 8, c = 20, d = -4,** calculate the value of:

1) $2(a + b) - c$ — Substitute in your numbers
$= 2(3 + 8) - 20$ — Work out the bracket first
$= 2 \times 11 - 20$ — Then the multiplication
$= 22 - 20$ — Then the subtraction
$= 2$

2) $3d^2 + c$ — Substitute in your numbers
$= 3 \times (-4)^2 + 20$ — Work out the square first ($- \times - = +$)
$= 3 \times 16 + 20$ — Then the multiplication
$= 48 + 20$ — Then the addition
$= 68$

3) $\dfrac{c(d + 1)}{5}$ — Substitute in your numbers
$= \dfrac{20(-4 + 1)}{5}$ — Work out the bracket first
$= \dfrac{20 \times -3}{5}$ — Then the multiplication ($+ \times - = -$)
$= \dfrac{-60}{5}$ — Then the division ($- \div + = -$)
$= -12$

4) $2a^3$ — Substitute in your numbers
$= 2 \times (3)^3$ — Work out the cube first
$= 2 \times 27$ — Then the multiplication
$= 54$

ALGEBRA

Brackets and Factorisation

Multiplying Out Brackets

When we multiply out a bracket, everything which is inside the bracket must be multiplied by whatever is immediately outside the bracket.

Examples ...

1) $4(x+3)$
$= 4 \times x + 4 \times 3$
$= 4x + 12$

2) $6(3x + 2)$
$= 6 \times 3x + 6 \times 2$
$= 18x + 12$

3) $4(5x - 4)$
$= 4 \times 5x + 4 \times -4$
$= 20x - 16$

4) $5(2x + 7)$
$= 5 \times 2x + 5 \times 7$
$= 10x + 35$

5) $x(x + 3) - 7$
$= x \times x + x \times 3 - 7$
$= x^2 + 3x - 7$

Factorisation

This is the reverse process to multiplying out brackets. An expression is rewritten with a bracket by taking out the highest factor common to all the terms in the expression.

Examples ...

1) $4x + 6 = 2(2x + 3)$
... as **2** is the highest factor common to both **4** and **6**

2) $12x - 18 = 6(2x - 3)$
... as **6** is the highest factor common to both **12** and **18**

3) $4x - 12y = 4(x - 3y)$
... as **4** is the highest factor common to both **4** and **12**

4) $3x^2 + 8x = x(3x + 8)$
... as x is the highest factor common to both x^2 and x

To check each of the examples above multiply out each bracket. You should end up with the original expression.

Solving Linear Equations 1

Equations such as ...

$4x = 12$

$x + 3 = 7$

$2(x + 5) = 14$

... are all examples of linear equations since the highest power they contain is x^1 (i.e. x). Each of these linear equations can be solved to find the 'unknown' value of x by collecting all the x's on one side and all the numbers on the other side. The simplest linear equation would involve one operation to solve it. Most however require at least two operations.

Examples ...

1) $6x = 18$

$\dfrac{6x}{6} = \dfrac{18}{6}$

$x = 3$

- Divide both sides of the equation by **6** to leave just x on the left-hand side.

2) $3x - 5 = 19$

$3x - 5 + 5 = 19 + 5$

$\dfrac{3x}{3} = \dfrac{24}{3}$

$x = 8$

- Add **5** to both sides of the equation to remove the **-5** from the left-hand side.
- Divide both sides of the equation by **3** to leave just x on the left-hand side.

3) $18 = 4(x + 3)$

$18 = 4x + 12$

$18 - 12 = 4x + 12 - 12$

$\dfrac{6}{4} = \dfrac{4x}{4}$

$1.5 = x$

or $x = 1.5$

- Multiply out the bracket on the right-hand side.
- Subtract **12** from both sides of the equation to remove the **+12** on the right-hand side.
- Divide both sides of the equation by **4** to leave just x on the right-hand side.

4) $5(x + 6) = 20$

$5x + 30 = 20$

$5x + 30 - 30 = 20 - 30$

$\dfrac{5x}{5} = \dfrac{-10}{5}$

$x = -2$

- Multiply out the bracket on the left-hand side.
- Subtract **30** from both sides of the equation to remove the **+30** on the left-hand side.
- Divide both sides of the equation by **5** to leave just x on the left-hand side.

Solving Linear Equations 2

The following examples have the 'unknown' e.g. x, appearing on both sides of the equation. Once again they are solved by collecting all the x's on one side and all the numbers on the other side.

It does not really matter on which side of the equal sign you collect all the x's, it is your choice. In the examples below, they are collected on the side that has the most positive x's to start with. This ensures you end up with a value for x rather than $-x$.

Examples ...

1
$$8x - 7 = 5x + 2$$
$$8x - 5x - 7 = 5x - 5x + 2$$
$$3x - 7 + 7 = 2 + 7$$
$$\frac{3x}{3} = \frac{9}{3}$$
$$x = 3$$

- Subtract **5x** from both sides of the equation to leave all the x's on the left-hand side.
- Add **7** to both sides of the equation to remove the **-7** on the left-hand side.
- Divide both sides of the equation by **3** to leave just x on the left-hand side.

2
$$4(3x - 2) = 14x + 4$$
$$12x - 8 = 14x + 4$$
$$12x - 12x - 8 = 14x - 12x + 4$$
$$-8 - 4 = 2x + 4 - 4$$
$$\frac{-12}{2} = \frac{2x}{2}$$
$$-6 = x$$
or $x = -6$

- Multiply out the bracket on the left-hand side.
- Subtract **12x** from both sides of the equation to leave all the x's on the right-hand side.
- Subtract **4** from both sides of the equation to remove the **+4** on the right-hand side.
- Divide both sides of the equation by **2** to leave just x on the right-hand side.

Problem Solving Using Linear Equations

This involves being given information, forming a linear equation from the information given and then solving the equation.

Example ...

The four angles of a quadrilateral are: **a, a + 20°, a + 40° and a + 60°**. Calculate the size of each angle.

Firstly ... we know that the angles of a quadrilateral add up to **360°**. Therefore ...

$$a + (a + 20) + (a + 40) + (a + 60) = 360$$
$$4a + 120 = 360$$
$$4a = 240 \quad \leftarrow \text{Subtract 120 from both sides}$$
$$a = 60° \quad \leftarrow \text{Divide both sides by 4}$$

$a = 60°$, $a + 20° = 80°$, $a + 40° = 100°$, $a + 60° = 120°$.

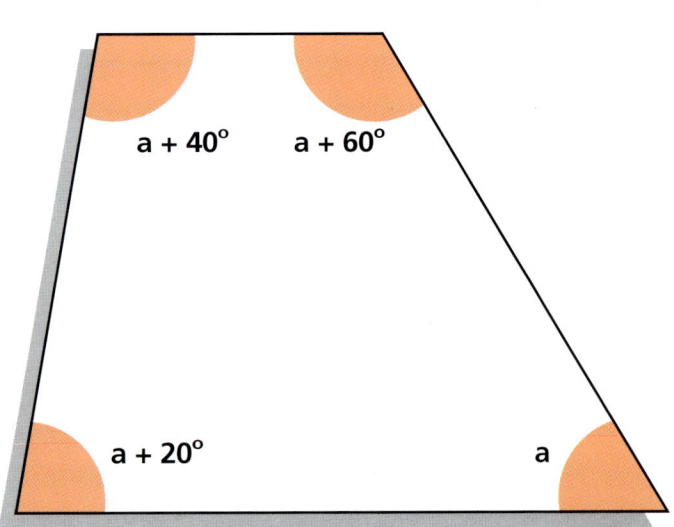

Formulae 1

Formulae show the relationship between two or more changeable quantities. They can be written in words, but most often symbols are used instead. For example, the area of a circle is given by the formula: **$A = \pi r^2$**, which describes the relationship between the area of a circle and its radius.

Rearranging Formulae

This simply means making a different letter the 'subject' of the formula, e.g. **a = b + c** has **a** as the subject since it is on one side by itself. If we wanted to make **b** or **c** the subject then we would need to rearrange the formula by moving terms from one side of the equal sign to the other. The processes involved are the same as solving linear equations (see previous two pages).

Examples ...

1 Make **b** the subject of the following formula. $a = b + c$ $a - c = b + \cancel{c} - \cancel{c}$ or $b = a - c$	- SUBTRACT **c** from both sides of the formula. This will remove the **+c** on the right-hand side to leave **b** on its own. - REWRITE the formula with **b** on the left-hand side.
2 Make **y** the subject of the following formula. $x + y = 7$ $\cancel{x} - \cancel{x} + y = 7 - x$ or $y = -x + 7$	- SUBTRACT **x** from both sides of the formula to remove the **x** on the left-hand side.
3 Make **x** the subject of the following formula. $4(3x + 2y) = 10$ $4 \times 3x + 4 \times 2y = 10$ $12x + 8y = 10$ $12x + \cancel{8y} - \cancel{8y} = 10 - 8y$ $\dfrac{\cancel{12}x}{\cancel{12}} = \dfrac{10 - 8y}{12}$ $x = \dfrac{10 - 8y}{12}$	- MULTIPLY out the bracket on the left-hand side. - SUBTRACT **8y** from both sides of the formula to remove the **+8y** on the left-hand side. - DIVIDE both sides of the formula by **12** to leave just **x** on the left-hand side.

Formulae 2

Using Formulae

Examples ...

1 A company hires a temporary member of staff. If the temp works 32 hours at a rate per hour of £6, calculate the cost of hiring using the following formula:

wage earned = hours worked x rate per hour

Our formula is:
wage earned
= hours worked x rate per hour
= 32 hours x £6
= £192

All we have to do is substitute values into our formula.

2 The formula that converts a temperature reading from degrees Celsius (°C) into degrees Fahrenheit (°F) is: $F = \frac{9}{5}C + 32$
What is the temperature in degrees Fahrenheit if the temperature in degrees Celsius is 25°C?

Our formula is: $F = \frac{9}{5}C + 32$

$F = \frac{9}{5} \times 25 + 32$
$F = 45 + 32$
$F = 77°F$

*We now substitute into our formula a value for **C**, which is 25°C, to work out **F***

3 The area of a triangle is given by the formula:
$A = \frac{B \times H}{2}$

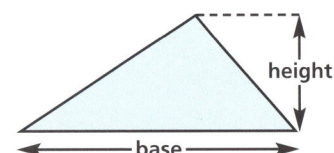

where **B** is length of base and **H** is height of triangle. Calculate the area of a triangle of height 6cm if the length of its base is 10cm.

Our formula is:
$A = \frac{B \times H}{2}$

$= \frac{10cm \times 6cm}{2}$

$= \frac{60}{2}$

$= 30cm^2$

*All we need to do is substitute values for **B** and **H** into our formula.*

Deriving Formulae

This means deriving a formula from given information. You may then need to use this formula to work out an unknown quantity. For example ...

Derive a formula for the perimeter of a rectangle in terms of its area, **A**, and width, **w**, only. Use it to work out the perimeter if area = 40cm² and width = 4cm

$\ell = \frac{A}{w}$
Perimeter = $2\ell + 2w$
width (w)
Length (ℓ)

Perimeter = $2\ell + 2w$

$= 2\frac{A}{w} + 2w$

$= \frac{2A}{w} + 2w$

$= \frac{2 \times 40}{4} + 2 \times 4$

$= \frac{80}{4} + 8$

$= 20 + 8$

$= 28cm$

*Firstly, we need to substitute $\frac{A}{w}$ for ℓ in our formula for perimeter, to give us the formula in terms of area and width only. All we do then is substitute in values for **A** and **w** to find the perimeter.*

Number Patterns & Sequences

A number pattern or sequence is a series of numbers which follow a rule. Each number in a sequence is called a **term** and has a position where the first number in the sequence is called the **1st term** and so on.

1st term	2nd term	3rd term	4th term		The next two terms
2,	6,	10,	14,...	The rule is that each term is **4 more** than the previous term i.e. they go up in fours.	...18, 22, ...
	+4	+4	+4		+4
20,	17,	14,	11,...	The rule is that each term is **3 less** than the previous term. i.e. they go down in threes.	...8, 5, ...
	-3	-3	-3		-3
1,	2,	4,	8, ...	The rule is that each term is **2 times** the previous term i.e. each term is two times bigger than the one before it.	...16, 32, ...
	x2	x2	x2		x2
1,	3,	9,	27,...	The rule is that each term is **3 times** the previous term i.e. each term is three times bigger than the one before it.	...81, 243,...
	x3	x3	x3		x3
1,	3,	7,	15,...	The rule is that each term is **twice** the previous term **plus one** i.e. each term is two times bigger than the one before it plus one.	...31, 63, ...
	(x2)+1	(x2)+1	(x2)+1		(x2)+1

A sequence can also be a series of diagrams.

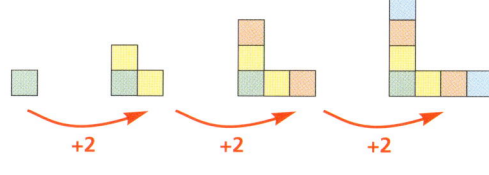

Each diagram (term) has **2 more** boxes in it than the previous diagram i.e. they go up in twos.

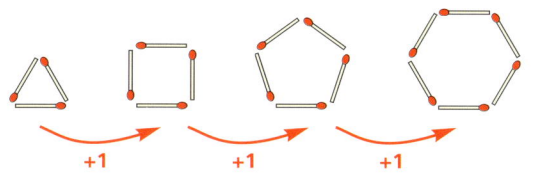

Each diagram (term) has **1 more** match in it than the previous diagram i.e. they go up in ones.

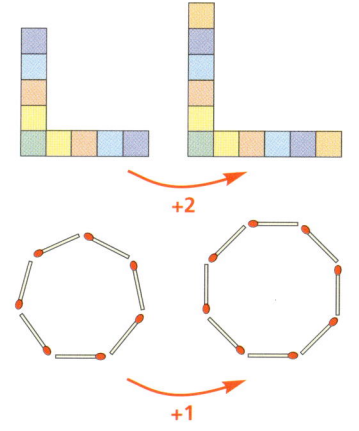

Plotting Points

All points are plotted on graph or squared paper. Usually your graph or squared paper is divided into four sections called **quadrants** by two lines known as the **x-axis**, which is a horizontal line, and the **y-axis**, which is a vertical line. The point where the two axes cross is called the **origin** (0,0).

The position of any plotted point is given by its **coordinates**. All coordinates are written as two numbers separated by a comma in a bracket e.g. (3,4) (5,-2), where ...

- The first number represents the **x** coordinate which is read going across horizontally to the right or left.
- The second number represents the **y** coordinate which is read vertically going up or down.

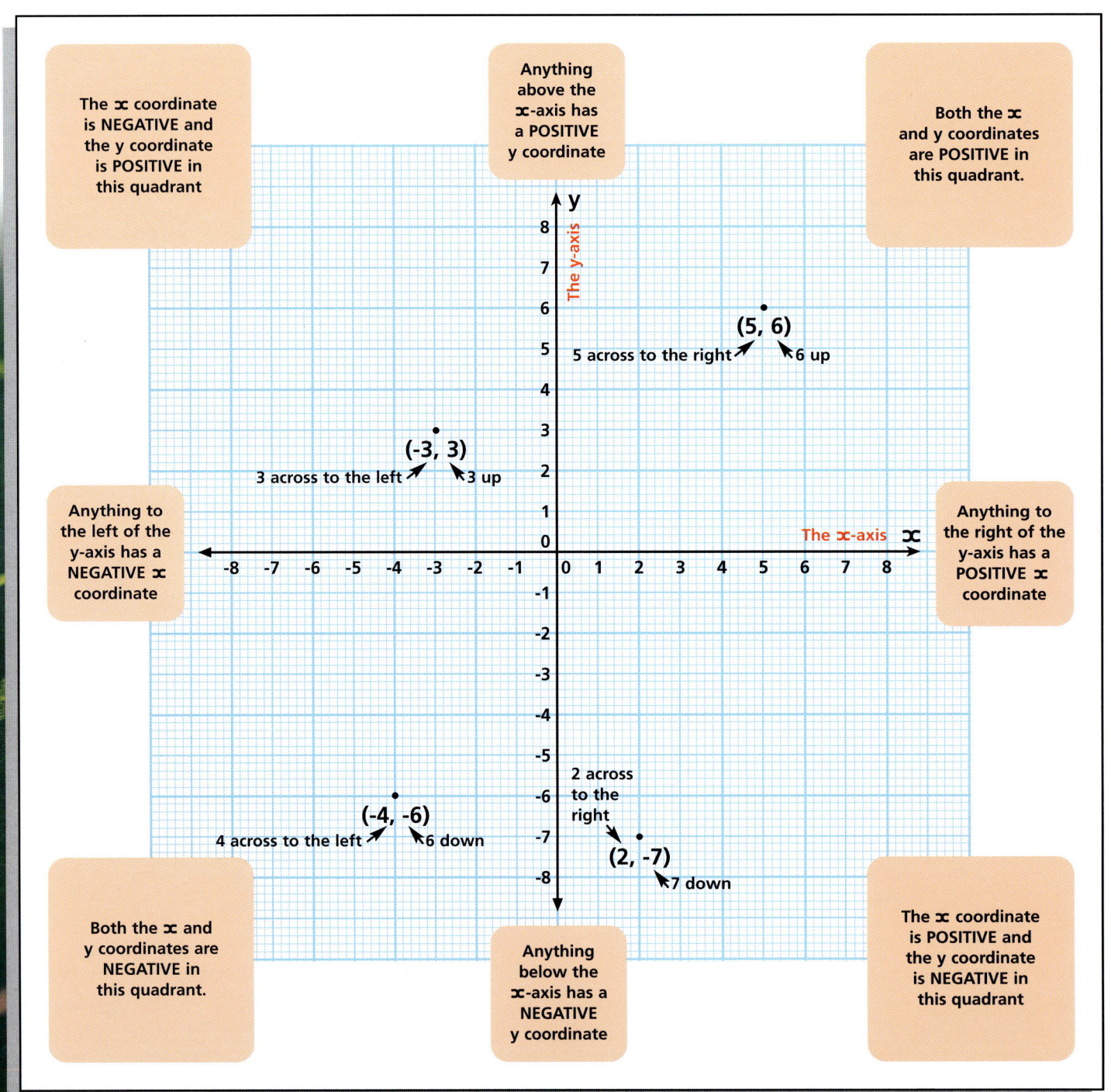

Graphs of Linear Functions 1

A linear function e.g. $y = x$, $y = 2x - 1$, $y = 0.5x + 1$ (i.e. a function in which the highest power of x is x^1), will always give you a straight line graph when drawn. To draw the graph of a linear function you only need to plot three points.

Your straight line must pass through all 3 points! If it doesn't then one of your points is wrong. You can either check your table again or better still work out the coordinates of another point.

Examples ...

1 Draw the graph of $y = 2x - 1$ for values of x between **-2** and **2**.

Firstly, we need to pick 3 values of x within the range, so that we can work out their y values. The two extreme values of x and one in the middle will do. Make up a table of results as follows:

Table of results for $y = 2x - 1$

x	-2	0	2
$2x$	(2 x -2 =) -4	(2 x 0 =) 0	(2 x 2 =) 4
-1	-1	-1	-1
$y = 2x - 1$	(-4 - 1 =) **-5**	(0 - 1 =) **-1**	(4 - 1 =) **3**

We now have the coordinates of 3 points: (-2,-5), (0,-1) and (2,3) and can plot our graph.

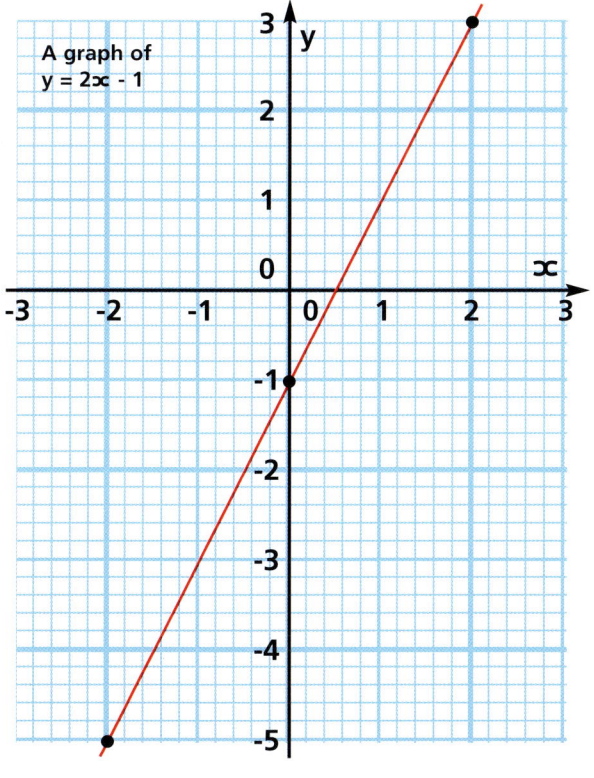

2 Draw the graph of $y = -0.5x + 2$ for values of x between **-2** and **2**.

Again we need to pick 3 values of x within the range, so that we can work out their y values. The two extreme values of x and one in the middle will do. Make up a table of results.

Table of results for $y = -0.5x + 2$

x	-2	0	2
$-0.5x$	(-0.5 x -2 =) 1	(-0.5 x 0 =) 0	(-0.5 x 2 =) -1
+ 2	+ 2	+ 2	+ 2
$y = -0.5x + 2$	(1 + 2 =) **3**	(0 + 2 =) **2**	(-1 + 2 =) **1**

We now have the coordinates of 3 points: (-2,3), (0,2) and (2,1) and can plot our graph.

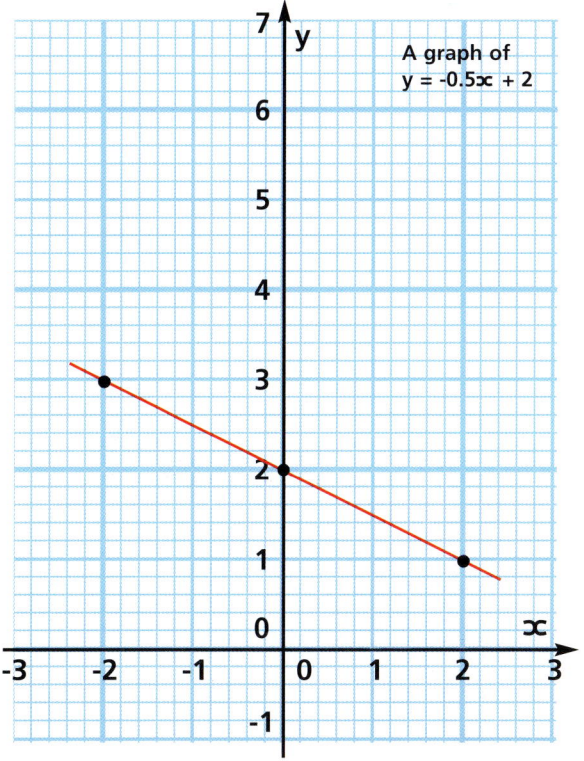

Graphs of Linear Functions 2

You may also be asked to plot the graph of a linear function where the first thing you have to do is rearrange the function to make **y** the subject. When you have done that you can then make up a table of results and plot your graph.

Examples ...

1 Draw the graph of **y - 2x = 1** for values of **x** between **-2** and **2**.

$$y - 2x = 1$$
$$y - 2x + 2x = 1 + 2x$$
$$y = 2x + 1$$

Add 2x to both sides to leave just y on the left-hand side

Table of results for y = 2x + 1

x	-2	0	2
2x	(2 x -2 =) -4	(2 x 0 =) 0	(2 x 2 =) 4
+1	+1	+1	+1
y = 2x + 1	(-4 + 1 =) -3	(0 + 1 =) 1	(4 + 1 =) 5

We now have the coordinates of 3 points: (-2,-3), (0,1) and (2,5) and can plot our graph.

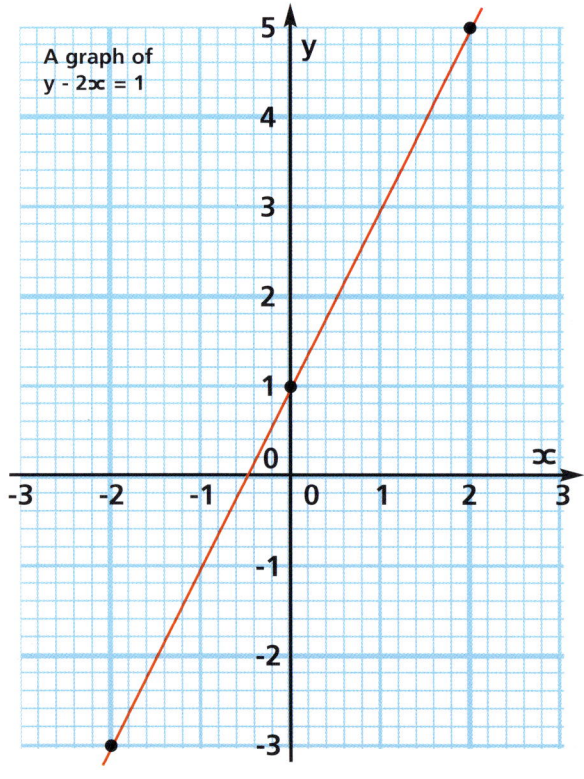

A graph of y - 2x = 1

2 Draw the graph of **x + y = 3** for values of **x** between **-2** and **2**.

$$x + y = 3$$
$$x - x + y = 3 - x$$
$$y = -x + 3$$

Subtract x from both sides to leave just y on the left-hand side

Table of results for y = -x + 3

x	-2	0	2
-x	(--2 =) 2	(-0 =) 0	(-2 =) -2
+3	+3	+3	+3
y = -x + 3	(2 + 3 =) 5	(0 + 3 =) 3	(-2 + 3 =) 1

We now have the coordinates of 3 points: (-2,5), (0,3) and (2,1) and can plot our graph.

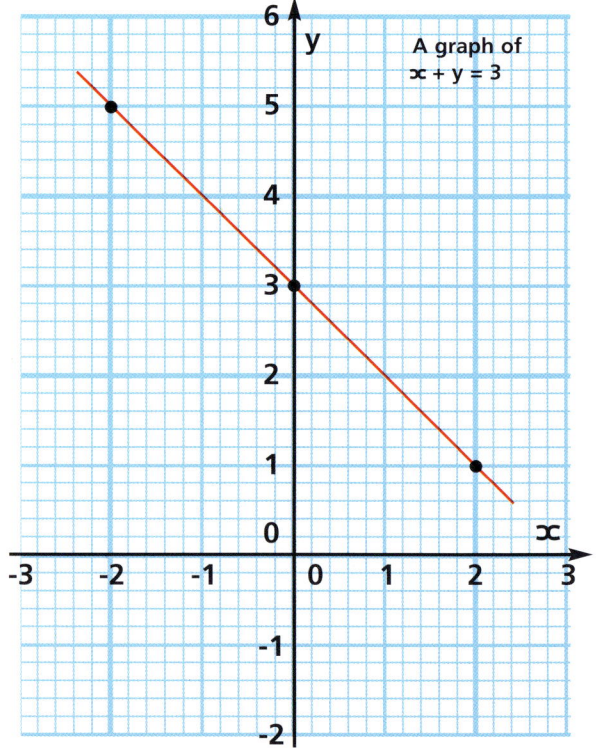

A graph of x + y = 3

Other Graphs 1

Graphs that Describe Real Life Situations

Example ...

The table below shows the prices charged by a car hire firm.

Fixed Charge £20
Cost per day £10

a) What is the relationship between cost of hire and number of days hire?

b) Draw a table to show cost of hire up to 7 days and then a graph to show the relationship between cost of hire and number of days hire.

a) Using the information given, the relationship is ...

Cost of hire = Fixed charge + (Cost per day x Number of days hire)

If we now substitute our fixed charge and cost per day into the relationship ...

Cost of hire (£) = 20 + (10 x Number of days hire)

b) We can now draw a table to show the cost of hire for up to 7 days ...

Number of days hire	1	2	3	4	5	6	7
Cost of hire (£) = 20 + (10 x Number of days hire)	20+(10x1)= 30	20+(10x2)= 40	20+(10x3)= 50	20+(10x4)= 60	20+(10x5)= 70	20+(10x6)= 80	20+(10x7)= 90

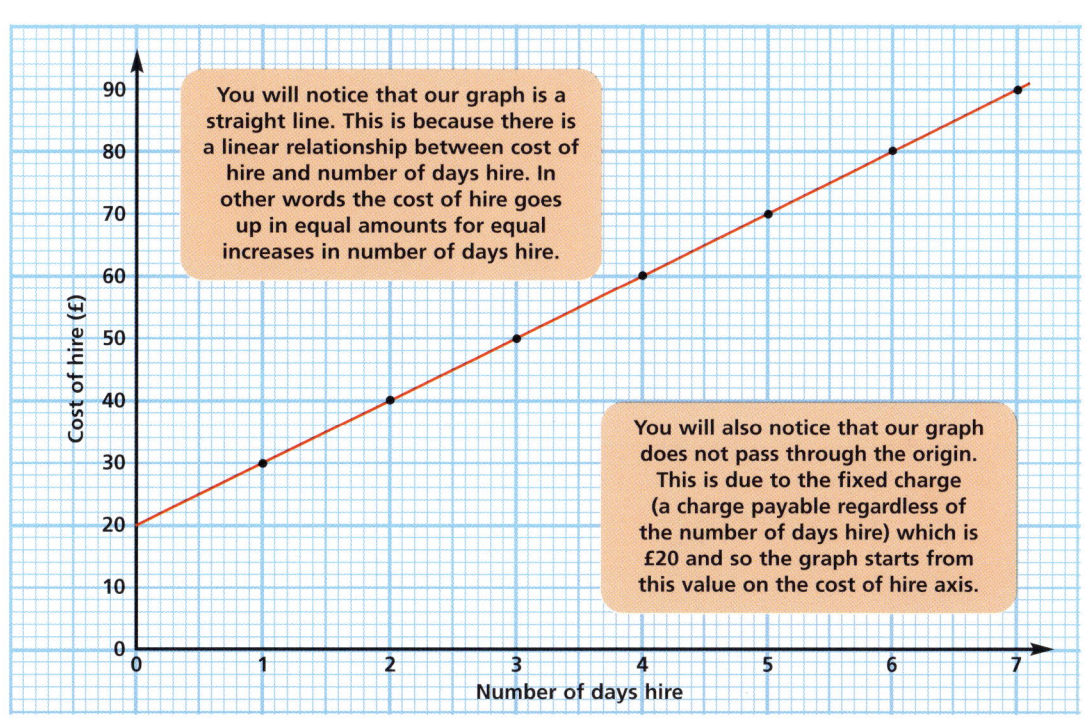

You will notice that our graph is a straight line. This is because there is a linear relationship between cost of hire and number of days hire. In other words the cost of hire goes up in equal amounts for equal increases in number of days hire.

You will also notice that our graph does not pass through the origin. This is due to the fixed charge (a charge payable regardless of the number of days hire) which is £20 and so the graph starts from this value on the cost of hire axis.

ALGEBRA

Other Graphs 2

Conversion Graphs

These are used to convert values of one quantity into another e.g. pounds sterling (£) into euros (€) or any other currency, miles into kilometres and so on.

Example

Draw a conversion graph for pounds sterling and euros up to £30 if £1 = €1.60. From your graph convert ...

a) £17 into euros
b) €40 into pounds sterling

Before we can draw our graph we need a table of values for pounds sterling and euros.

Pounds sterling (£)	10	20	30
Euros (€)	(10x1.6=) 16	(20x1.6=) 32	(30x1.6=) 48

a) Go to £17 on the pounds sterling axis, draw a dotted line across (→) to the graph and then down (↓) to the euros axis. **£17 = €27.**

b) Go to €40 on the euros axis, draw a dotted line up (↑) to the graph and then across (←) to the pounds sterling axis. **€40 = £25.**

Other Examples ...

Here are 6 other examples (there are numerous others) where a graph can be used to show a real life situation.

All of these graphs require common sense in their interpretation as each one is very different.

Temperature at different times in the day

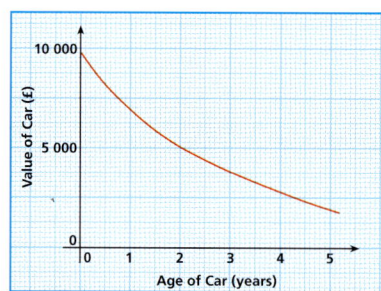
Value of a car as it gets older

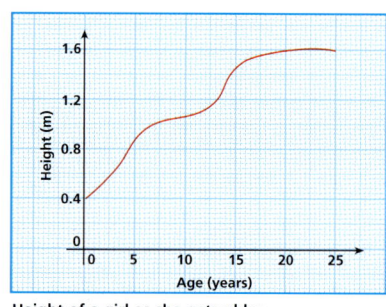
Height of a girl as she gets older

Weight of a man as he gets older

Pulse rate of a runner after the race is over

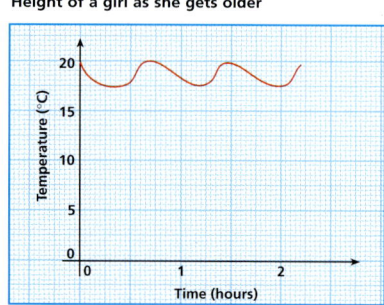
Temperature of a thermostatically controlled room over a period of time

Other Graphs 3

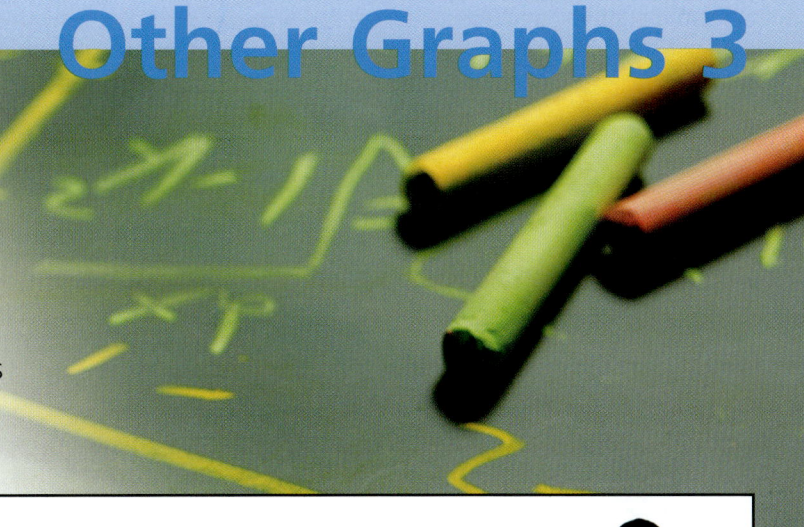

Distance - Time Graphs

These are also known as travel graphs, where distance is always plotted on the vertical axis and time is always plotted on the horizontal axis. For a distance-time graph the slope or gradient is always equal to the speed. If there is no slope, there is no movement i.e. speed = 0.

Example ...

A boy sets off from home riding his bike to go to a friend's house. A distance-time graph of his journey is shown below. Describe his movement between **a)** O and A, **b)** A and B and **c)** B and C.

a) Between O and A the boy is cycling with constant speed given by the slope or gradient.

$$\text{Speed} = \frac{\text{Distance}}{\text{Time}}$$

$$= \frac{\text{Distance cycled from O to A}}{\text{Time taken to cycle from O to A}}$$

$$= \frac{5\text{km}}{0.5\text{h}} = 10\text{km/h}$$

b) Between A and B there is no movement i.e. the boy has stopped cycling for 1 hour.
Speed = 0 since there is no slope or gradient.

c) Between B and C the boy is again cycling with constant speed given by the slope or gradient.

$$\text{Speed} = \frac{\text{Distance}}{\text{Time}}$$

$$= \frac{\text{Distance cycled from B to C}}{\text{Time taken to cycle from B to C}}$$

$$= \frac{2\text{km}}{1\text{h}}$$

$$= 2\text{km/h}$$

Angles 1

All angles are measured in DEGREES (°). A protractor can be used to measure the size of an angle.

Acute, Right, Obtuse and Reflex Angles

An angle LESS THAN 90° is called an ACUTE ANGLE

An angle EQUAL TO 90° is called a RIGHT ANGLE

An angle GREATER THAN 90° but LESS THAN 180° is called an OBTUSE ANGLE

An angle GREATER THAN 180° is called a REFLEX ANGLE

Angles on a Straight Line, at a Point and Vertically Opposite

Angles on a straight line add up to 180° (also known as Adjacent Angles)

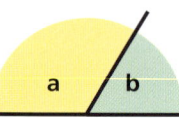

a = 120°
b = 60°   a + b = 180°

p = 45°
q = 90°   p + q + r = 180°
r = 45°

Angles at a point add up to 360°

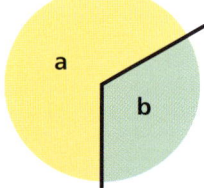

a = 240°
b = 120°   a + b = 360°

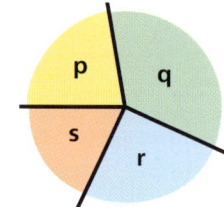

p = 80°
q = 125°
r = 90°   p + q + r + s = 360°
s = 65°

Vertically opposite angles are equal

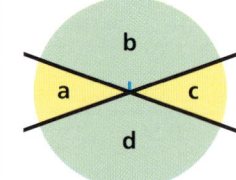

a = 40° } Vertically opposite
c = 40°
b = 140° } Vertically opposite
d = 140°

Examples ...

1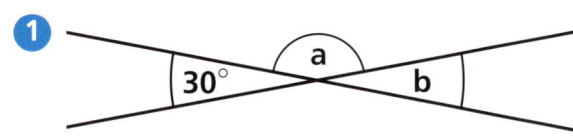

a = 180° − 30° = 150°
(Angles on a straight line add up to 180°)
b = 30° (Vertically opposite angles are equal)

2 c = 360° − (120° + 160°)
c = 360° − 280° = 80°
(Angles at a point add up to 360°)

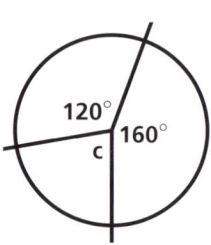

Angles 2

Parallel Lines

Remember that parallel lines run in exactly the same direction and never meet. Parallel lines are shown by arrows on the lines concerned. There is no limit to the number of lines which may run parallel to each other. When a straight line crosses two or more parallel lines, corresponding, alternate and allied angles are formed.

Alternate Angles

- Alternate angles are formed on opposite (alternate) sides of a line which crosses two or more parallel lines.
- Alternate angles are always equal in size.
- Alternate angles can be easily spotted because they form a letter **Z** (although sometimes it may be reversed, **Ƨ**!!).

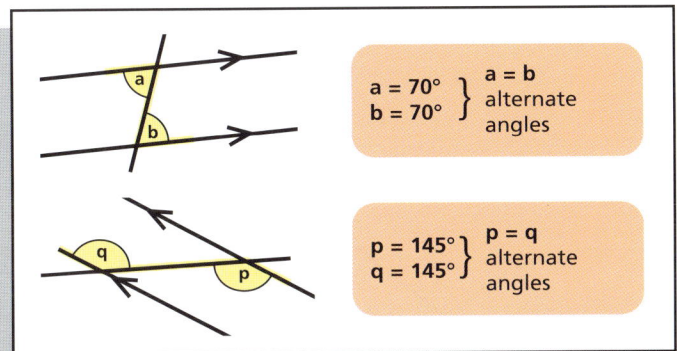

Corresponding Angles

- Corresponding angles are formed on the same side of a line, which crosses two or more parallel lines. They all appear in matching (corresponding) positions above or below the parallel lines.
- Corresponding angles are always equal in size.
- Corresponding angles can be easily spotted because they form a letter **F** (although sometimes it may be reversed, **ꟻ**, or upside down **Ⅎ,ꟻ**!!)

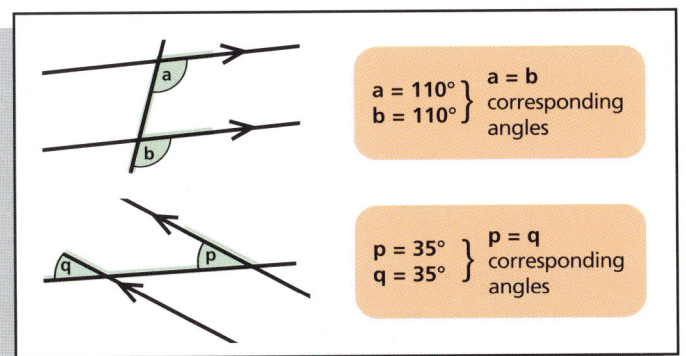

Allied Angles

- Allied angles are formed on the same side of a line, which crosses two or more parallel lines. They appear inside two parallel lines, facing each other.
- Allied angles always add up to 180°.
- Allied angles can be easily spotted because they form a letter **⊏** or **⊔** (although sometimes it may be reversed, **⊐** or **⊓**!!).

* Allied angles do not appear on the course specification. They are included here because they will help you to understand the relationships between the different angles formed when a straight line crosses two or more parallel lines. You will find them useful when calculating angles too!

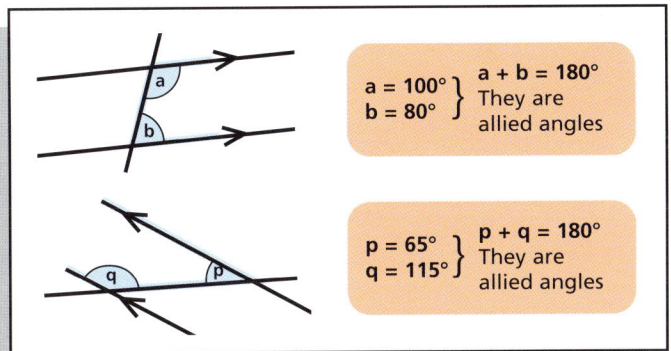

Example

Calculate the angles **a**, **b**, and **c** in relation to x in the following parallelogram.

$x + 100° = 180°$ ← angles on a straight line

so, $x = 80°$

$a = x$ ← corresponding angles

so, $a = 80°$

$b = x$ ← alternate angles

so, $b = 80°$

$c + x = 180°$ ← allied angles

so, $c = 100°$

Triangles

A triangle is a 3 sided two-dimensional shape. The interior angles of the triangle below are **a**, **b** and **c**.

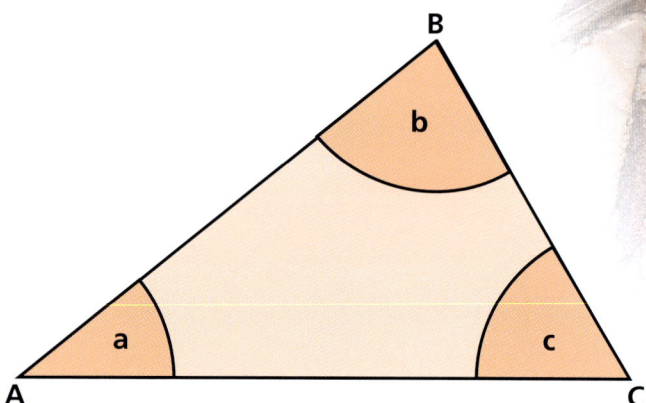

If we extend the side **AC** to point **D**, and add a line from **C** to **E** which runs parallel to **AB** then we get the following diagram.

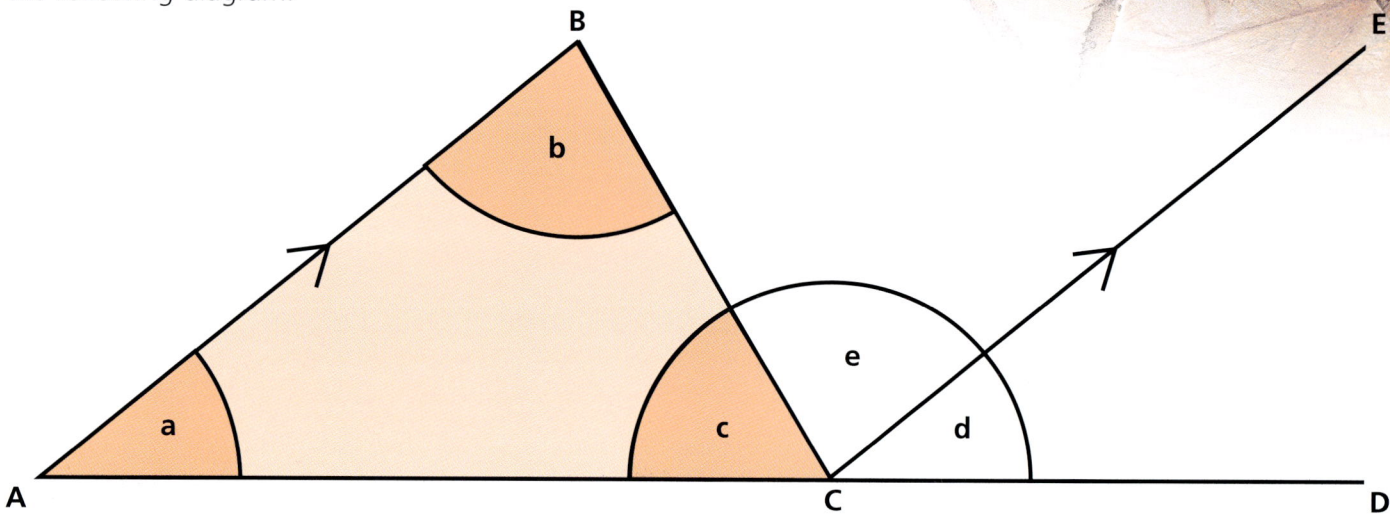

We can now say the following things about these particular angles:

❶ The Interior Angles of a Triangle add up to 180°

From our diagram …
- e = b   ← alternate angles
- d = a   ← corresponding angles

However …
- c + e + d = 180°   ← angles on a straight line add up to 180°

Therefore …
- c + b + a = 180°, which proves that …

THE INTERIOR ANGLES OF A TRIANGLE ADD UP TO 180°

❷ The Exterior Angle of a Triangle is equal to the sum of the Interior Angles at the other two vertices

The exterior angle of this triangle at the vertex (corner) C is angle BCD. However we have already shown that:

- e = b   ← alternate angles
- d = a   ← corresponding angles

Therefore **d + e = a + b**, which proves that …

THE EXTERIOR ANGLE OF A TRIANGLE IS EQUAL TO THE SUM OF THE INTERIOR ANGLES AT THE OTHER TWO VERTICES.

Types of Triangle

Right-angled triangles
- One angle is equal to 90°.

Equilateral triangles
- All sides are equal in length.
- All the angles are equal to 60°.

Isosceles triangles
- Two sides only are equal in length.
- Two angles only are equal in size (angles opposite the equal sides). These are usually referred to as the base angles.

Scalene triangles
- This is the name given to triangles which have no equal sides and no equal angles.

Example ...

The following diagram shows an isosceles and a right-angled triangle. Calculate the angles **a** to **f** explaining your reasoning.

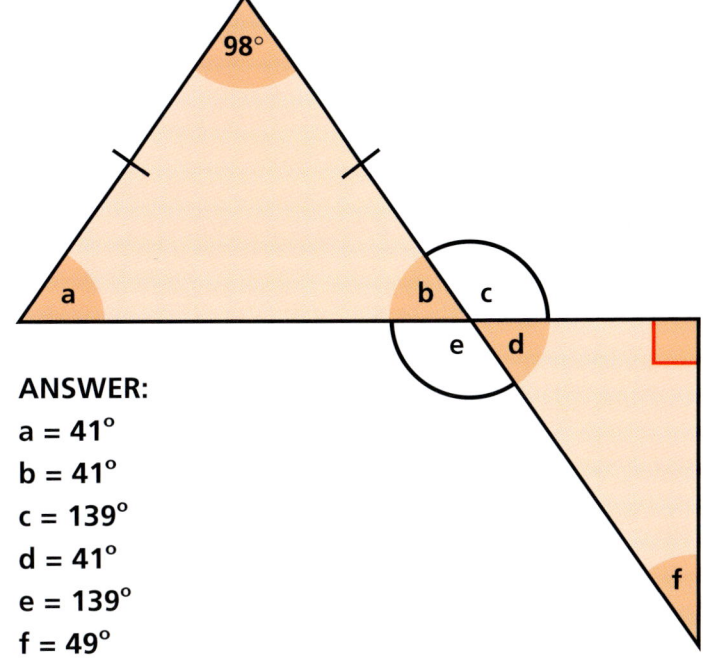

$a = b$ (Base angles of an isosceles triangle)
But, $a + b + 98° = 180°$ (Interior angles of a triangle)
so, $a + b = 82°$ so each one is equal to **41°**.
$b + c = 180°$ (Angles on a straight line)
$c = 180° - 41° = 139°$
$b = d$ (Vertically opposite angles) so, $d = 41°$
$c = e$ (Vertically opposite angles) so, $e = 139°$
$d + f +$ right-angle $= 180°$
(Interior angles of a triangle)
so, $f = 180° - 90° - 41° = 49°$

ANSWER:
a = 41°
b = 41°
c = 139°
d = 41°
e = 139°
f = 49°

SHAPE, SPACE & MEASURES

Quadrilaterals

A quadrilateral is a 4 sided, two-dimensional shape which has interior angles that add up to 360°.

Types of Quadrilateral

Square		• All the sides are equal in length • Opposite sides are parallel • All the angles are equal to 90° • Diagonals are equal and bisect each other at right-angles. • Diagonals also bisect each of the interior angles.
Parallelogram		• Opposite sides are equal in length • Opposite sides are parallel • Opposite angles are equal in size • Diagonals bisect each other.
Rhombus		• All the sides are equal in length • Opposite sides are parallel • Opposite angles are equal in size • Diagonals bisect each other at right-angles • Diagonals also bisect the interior angles.
Rectangle		• Opposite sides are equal in length • Opposite sides are parallel • All the angles are equal to 90° • Diagonals are equal and bisect each other.
Trapezium		• No sides equal in length • One pair of sides parallel • No angles equal in size
Kite		• 2 pairs of equal adjacent sides • 1 pair of opposite equal angles • Diagonals cross at right-angles and one bisects the other.

The Interior Angles of a Quadrilateral

In this quadrilateral ...
  $a = 63°$, $b = 106°$, $c = 145°$, $d = 46°$
If we add these together ...
  $63° + 106° + 145° + 46° = 360°$

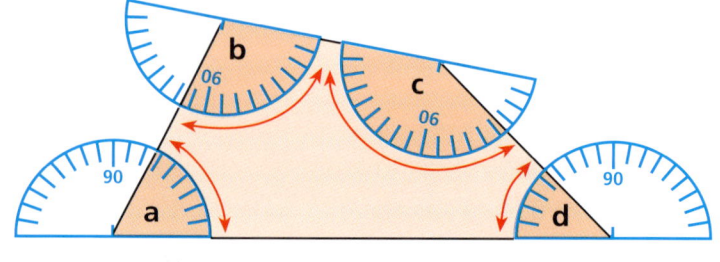

This is true of all quadrilaterals and can be proved by dividing the quadrilateral into 2 triangles:
  $p + q + r = 180°$ (Interior angles of a triangle)
  $s + t + u = 180°$ (Interior angles of a triangle)
The sum of the interior angles of the quadrilateral is
  $(p + s) + q + (r + t) + u$ which is therefore equal to
  $(p + q + r) + (s + t + u)$
i.e. $180° + 180° = 360°$

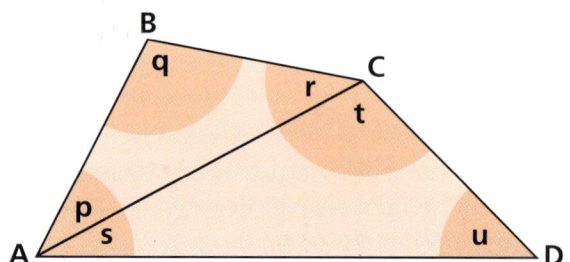

Irregular Polygons

Polygons

A polygon is a 3 or more sided two-dimensional shape. We have already seen the 3 sided polygon (triangle) and the 4 sided polygon (quadrilateral). A polygon is said to be REGULAR if all its sides and all its angles are equal. Otherwise it is known as an IRREGULAR polygon. Take a look at the two irregular polygons below.

Interior and Exterior Angles of a Polygon

The angles inside a polygon are called the INTERIOR ANGLES and those outside are called the EXTERIOR ANGLES. As for triangles and quadrilaterals the size of each of these angles can be measured using a protractor.

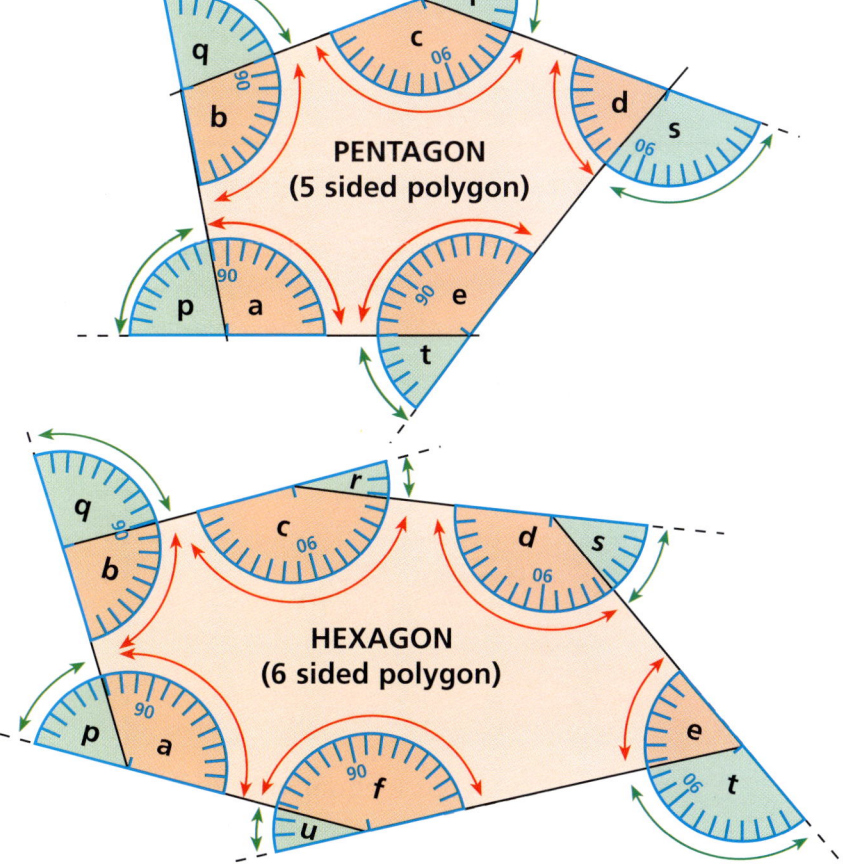

Interior angles	Exterior angles	Interior + Exterior angles
a = 100°	p = 80°	a + p = 180°
b = 100°	q = 80°	b + q = 180°
c = 140°	r = 40°	c + r = 180°
d = 70°	s = 110°	d + s = 180°
e = 130°	t = 50°	e + t = 180°
a+b+c+d+e = 540°	p+q+r+s+t = 360°	

Interior angles	Exterior angles	Interior + Exterior angles
a = 121°	p = 59°	a + p = 180°
b = 89°	q = 91°	b + q = 180°
c = 158°	r = 22°	c + r = 180°
d = 136°	s = 44°	d + s = 180°
e = 63°	t = 117°	e + t = 180°
f = 153°	u = 27°	f + u = 180°
a+b+c+d+e+f = 720°	p+q+r+s+t+u = 360°	

We can see from above that ...

1. **The Exterior Angles of a polygon always add up to 360°**
2. **The Interior Angle + the Exterior Angle always add up to 180°**

We can also see that the interior angles of different polygons do not add up to the same number of degrees. A triangle is 180°, a quadrilateral is 360°, a pentagon is 540°, a hexagon is 720°. The more sides the polygon has the greater the sum of the interior angles.

The sum of the interior angles
= (n - 2) x 180°
(where n = number of sides)

Name of Polygon	Number of sides (n)	Sum of Interior Angles, (n - 2) x 180°	Sum of Exterior Angles
Triangle	3	180°	360°
Quadrilateral	4	360°	360°
Pentagon	5	540°	360°
Hexagon	6	720°	360°

Regular Polygons

Regular Polygons

These are polygons that have ...
- **Sides of the same length**
- **Interior angles of the same size**
- **Exterior angles of the same size**

Here are four examples of regular polygons:

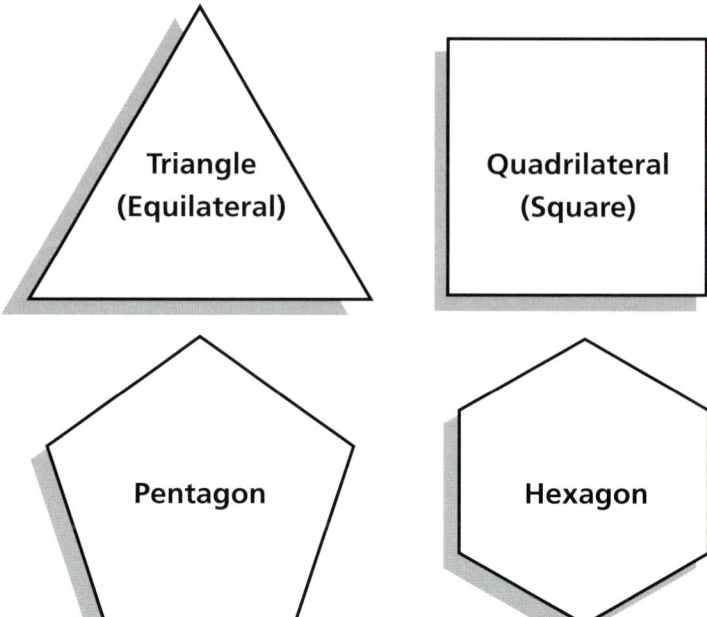

Knowing that the exterior angles of a polygon add up to 360°, that the interior angles are equal in a regular polygon and that the exterior and interior angles add up to 180° enables various calculations to be performed:

Examples ...

1) Calculate the size of **a)** each exterior and **b)** each interior angle for a regular hexagon (6 sides).

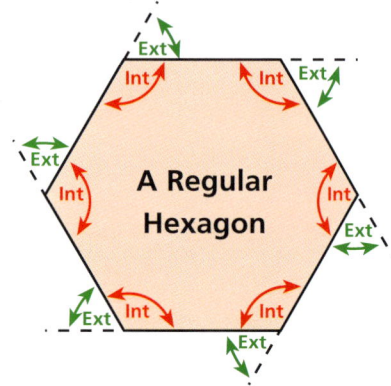

A Regular Hexagon has 6 equal Interior angles and 6 equal Exterior angles.

a) The Exterior angles of a Hexagon add up to 360° (see previous page)

Each Exterior Angle = $\frac{360°}{6}$ = 60°

b) The Interior angle + the Exterior angle add up to 180° (see previous page)

Each Interior Angle
= 180° - Exterior Angle
= 180° - 60° = 120°

2) A regular polygon has each interior angle = 108°. Calculate **a)** the size of each exterior angle, **b)** the number of sides the polygon has.

a) The Interior angle + the Exterior angle add up to 180°.

Each Exterior Angle
= 180° - Interior Angle
= 180° - 108° = 72°

b) The Exterior angles of a Polygon add up to 360° (see previous page)

Number of Exterior Angles = $\frac{360°}{72°}$ = 5

Number of sides = 5
(i.e. it is a regular PENTAGON)

Congruence and Tessellation

Congruent Shapes

These boys are IDENTICAL in their SIZE and SHAPE although their position relative to each other may be different. These four boys are congruent:

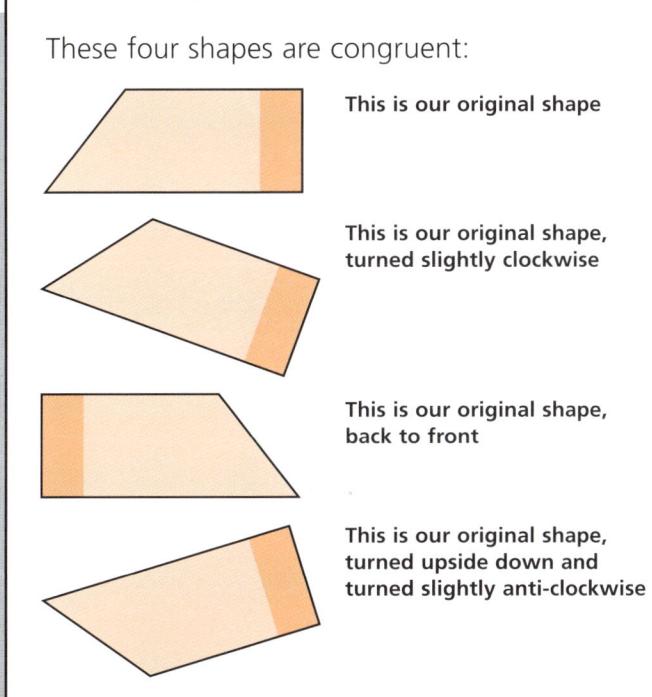

These four shapes are congruent:

This is our original shape

This is our original shape, turned slightly clockwise

This is our original shape, back to front

This is our original shape, turned upside down and turned slightly anti-clockwise

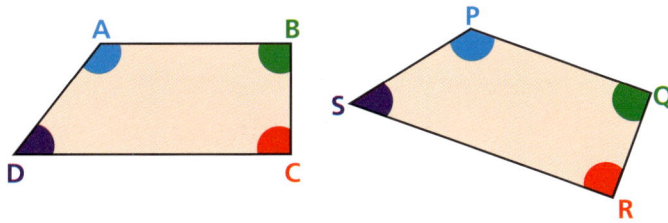

Shape ABCD and shape PQRS are CONGRUENT because $\hat{A} = \hat{P}$, $\hat{B} = \hat{Q}$, $\hat{C} = \hat{R}$ and $\hat{D} = \hat{S}$

TWO CONGRUENT SHAPES HAVE ANGLES THE SAME SIZE and also AB = PQ, BC = QR, CD = RS and DA = SP

TWO CONGRUENT SHAPES HAVE SIDES OF THE SAME LENGTH

Tessellations

A TESSELLATION is a pattern of CONGRUENT SHAPES that fit together with NO GAPS IN BETWEEN to cover a flat surface. Your kitchen floor may well be a tessellation. Not all congruent shapes form a tessellation.

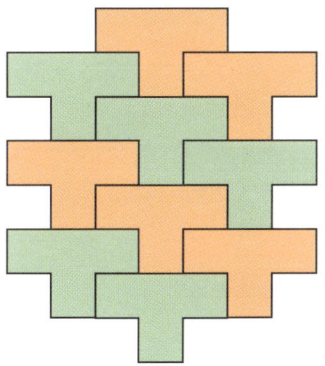

A tessellation can also be made using two or more congruent shapes.

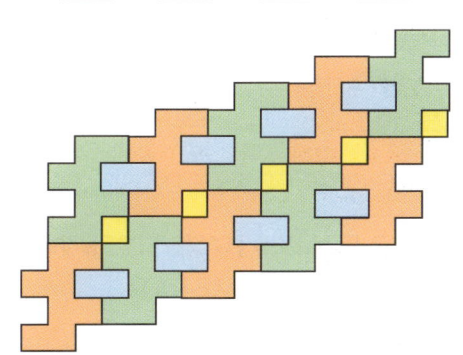

Similarity

Similar Shapes

These boys are IDENTICAL in their SHAPE but they are NOT IDENTICAL in SIZE (they can be bigger or smaller). Yet again their position relative to each other may be different. These four boys are SIMILAR:

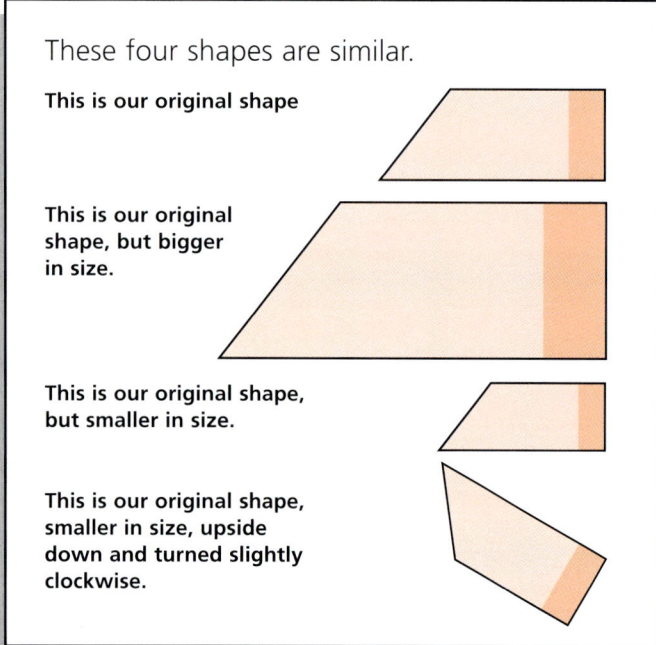

These four shapes are similar.

This is our original shape

This is our original shape, but bigger in size.

This is our original shape, but smaller in size.

This is our original shape, smaller in size, upside down and turned slightly clockwise.

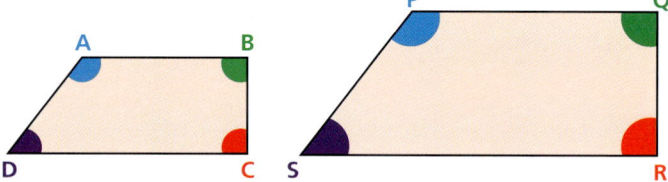

Shape ABCD and shape PQRS are SIMILAR because $\hat{A} = \hat{P}$, $\hat{B} = \hat{Q}$, $\hat{C} = \hat{R}$ and $\hat{D} = \hat{S}$

TWO SIMILAR SHAPES HAVE ANGLES THE SAME SIZE and also $\frac{AB}{PQ} = \frac{BC}{QR} = \frac{CD}{RS} = \frac{DA}{SP}$

or AB:PQ = BC:QR = CD:RS = DA:SP

TWO SIMILAR SHAPES HAVE SIDES WHOSE LENGTH ARE IN THE SAME RATIO.

Any two circles and any two squares are mathematically similar, while **in general**, two rectangles are not.

Example

The two triangles below are similar. Calculate the length of ...

a) QR

b) AC

In triangle **ABC**, $\hat{B} = 70°$ (180° − (60° + 50°)) and in triangle **PQR**, $\hat{R} = 60°$ (180° − (70° + 50°)) And so $\hat{A} = \hat{P}$, $\hat{B} = \hat{Q}$, $\hat{C} = \hat{R}$

This means that triangle **ABC** is similar to triangle **PQR** which means that ...

$$\frac{AB}{PQ} = \frac{BC}{QR} = \frac{AC}{PR}$$

$$\frac{9.2cm}{4.6cm} = \frac{8.4cm}{QR} = \frac{AC}{5cm}$$

Don't assume that the shapes (in this case triangles) are always lettered in alphabetical order

We can now calculate the unknown lengths ...

a) $\frac{9.2cm}{4.6cm} = \frac{8.4cm}{QR}$

$QR = \frac{8.4cm \times 4.6cm}{9.2cm}$

Rearranged to get QR on its own

$QR = 4.2cm$

b) $\frac{9.2cm}{4.6cm} = \frac{AC}{5cm}$

$AC = \frac{9.2cm \times 5cm}{4.6cm}$

Rearranged to get AC on its own

$AC = 10cm$

Transformations 1

Types of Transformation

A transformation is a process which changes the position (and possibly the size and orientation) of a shape. There are four different types of transformation: **reflection**, **rotation**, **translation**, **enlargement**.

❶ Reflection

A reflection in a line produces a mirror image in which corresponding points on the original shape and the mirror image are always the same distance from the mirror line. A line joining corresponding points always crosses the mirror line at 90°. To describe a reflection you must specify the MIRROR LINE by giving the equation of the line of reflection (in the examples on the right these are $x = 6$ and $y = 1$). As you can see, in a reflection, the ORIENTATION and POSITION changes but everything else stays the same. Therefore the image is congruent to the object under a reflection. Difficult reflections can be completed more easily if you use tracing paper. The example below is a reflection in the line $y = -1$.

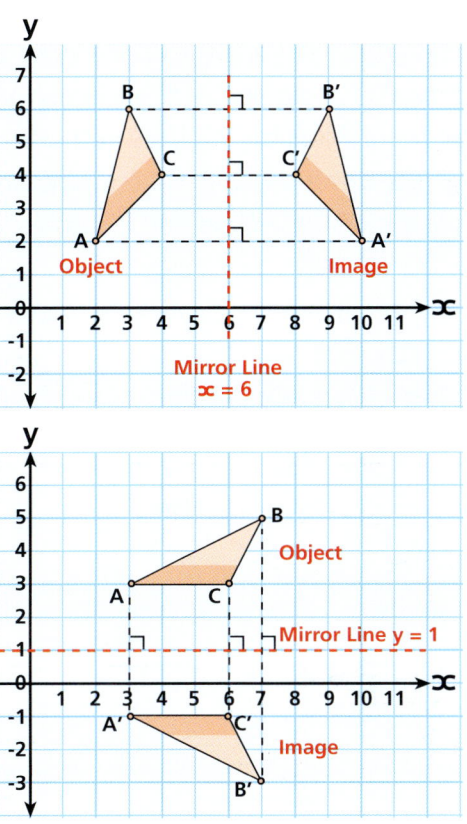

❶ Mark two points (● and ●) on your mirror line

❷ Draw in the mirror line, mark points and object carefully on the tracing paper, and then flip the tracing paper over (don't just rotate it!)...

❸ ...making sure that you line up the mirror line and marked points with the original. Mark in position of IMAGE.

❹ Remove the tracing paper. Draw in IMAGE and LABEL. An inverted comma (') after the label is used to denote a point on a reflected image.

Transformations 2

② Rotation

A rotation turns a shape through a clockwise or anti-clockwise angle about a fixed point known as the Centre of Rotation. All lines in the shape rotate through the same angle. Rotation, (just like reflection) changes the ORIENTATION and POSITION of the shape, but everything else stays the same.

Therefore the image is congruent to the object under a rotation. To describe a rotation, you must specify the following three things:
- The DIRECTION OF TURN (clockwise/anti-clockwise)
- The CENTRE OF ROTATION
- The AMOUNT TURNED.

Examples ...

Rotation of $\frac{1}{4}$ turn clockwise about the origin (0,0)

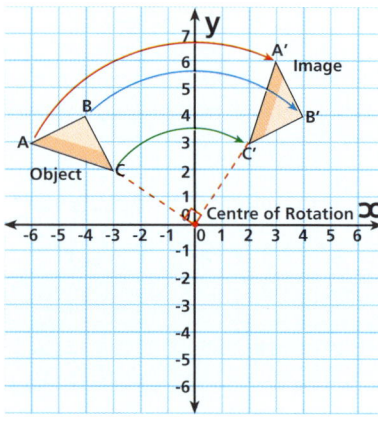

Rotation of $\frac{1}{2}$ turn clockwise about the origin (0,0)

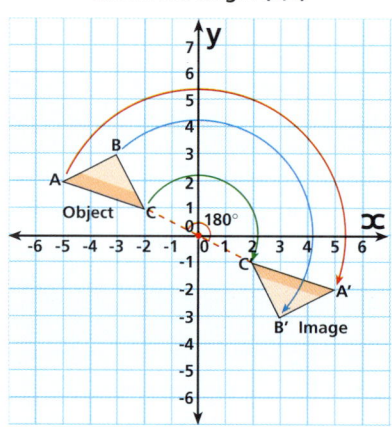

Rotation of $\frac{3}{4}$ turn clockwise about the origin (0,0) (is the same as a rotation of $\frac{1}{4}$ turn anti-clockwise)

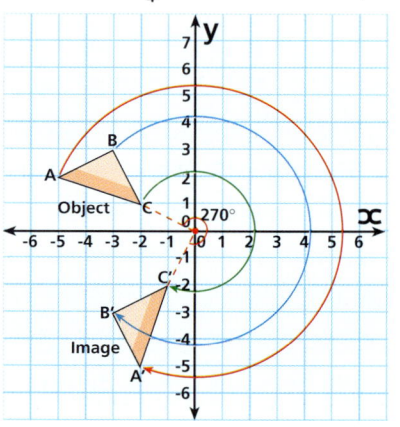

Difficult rotations can be completed more easily if you use tracing paper. If we wanted to rotate triangle ABC $\frac{1}{4}$ turn clockwise about the origin (0,0) ...

❶ Draw in axes and object carefully on the tracing paper

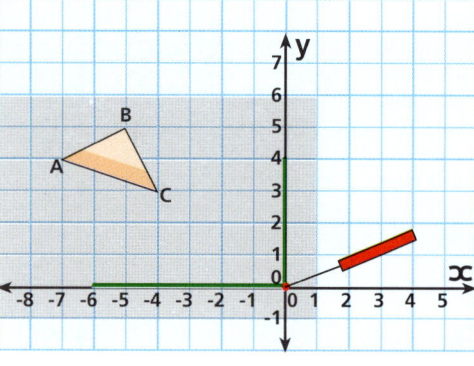

❷ Place point of compass on centre of rotation (0,0) and rotate paper clockwise

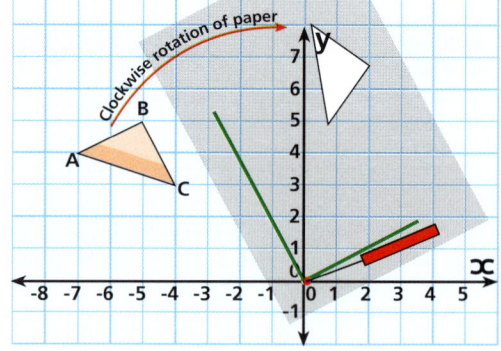

❸ After a $\frac{1}{4}$ turn mark in position of Image

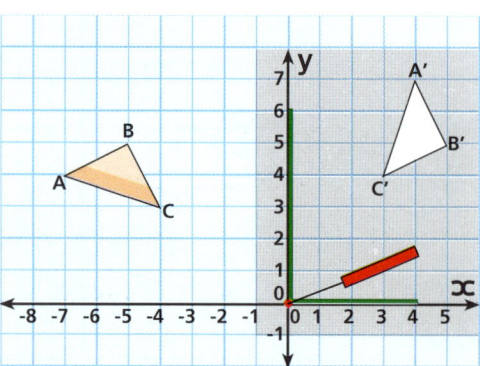

❹ Remove the tracing paper. Draw in image and label

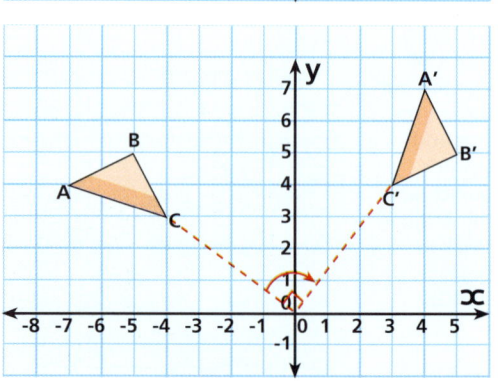

Transformations 3

3 Translation

A translation alters the position of a shape by moving every point of it by the same distance in the same direction. To describe a translation, you must specify the following two things:

- THE DIRECTION OF THE MOVEMENT
- THE DISTANCE MOVED

This can be summarised using brackets in which the movement in the **x** direction is placed directly above the movement in the **y** direction. Positive and negative numbers are used to indicate the direction of the movement. (See diagram alongside.) Translation only changes the POSITION of the shape. Everything else stays the same, so that any figure is congruent to its image under a translation.

Difficult translations can be completed more easily if you use tracing paper. Notice that all points (**P'**, **Q'**, **R'**, **S'**, **T'** and **U'**) in the example below have moved 6 to the right and 6 down.

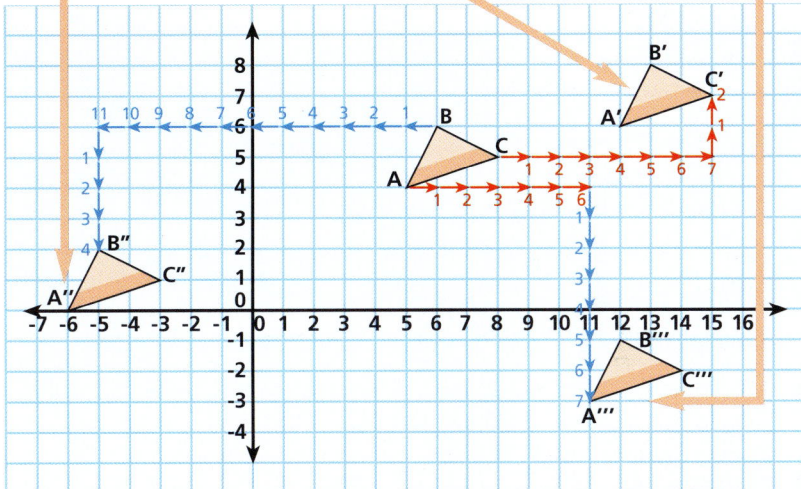

ABC has been translated to A''B''C'' by moving 11 squares to the left and then 4 squares down. This translation is written as $\binom{-11}{-4}$

ABC has been translated to A'B'C' by moving 7 squares to the right and then 2 squares up. This translation is written as $\binom{7}{2}$

ABC has been translated to A'''B'''C''' by moving 6 squares to the right and then 7 squares down. This translation is written as $\binom{6}{-7}$

- Movement to the right (→) or up (↑) is positive
- Movement to the left (←) or down (↓) is negative

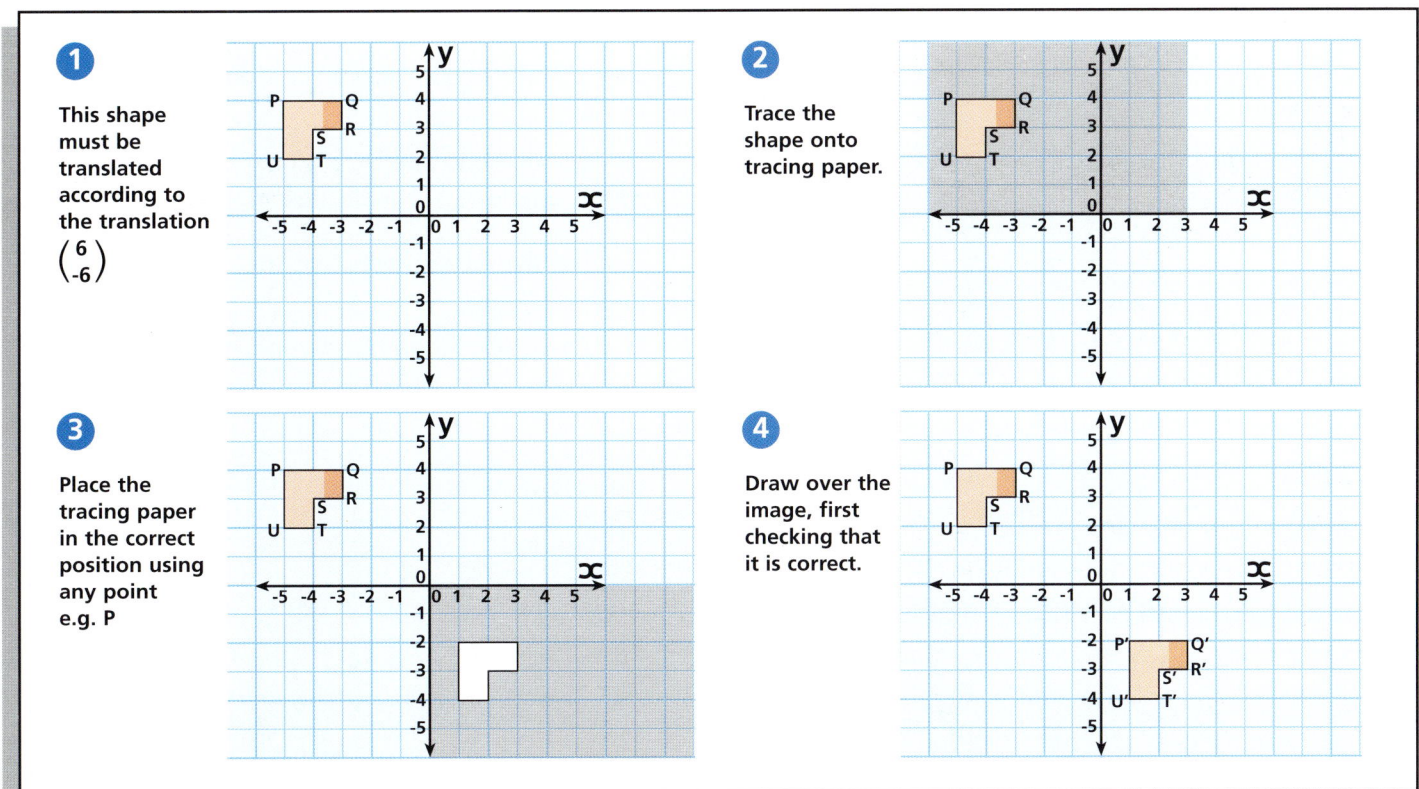

1 This shape must be translated according to the translation $\binom{6}{-6}$

2 Trace the shape onto tracing paper.

3 Place the tracing paper in the correct position using any point e.g. P

4 Draw over the image, first checking that it is correct.

Transformations 4

④ Enlargement

An enlargement changes the size of a shape. The shape can be made bigger or smaller according to the Scale Factor. All enlargements take place from one point called the Centre of Enlargement.

To describe an enlargement you must specify the following two things:
- THE CENTRE OF ENLARGEMENT
- A POSITIVE SCALE FACTOR

Scale Factor Greater Than 1

A Scale Factor greater than 1 means that the size of the image is bigger than the size of the object. Triangle A'B'C' is an enlargement of triangle ABC by a scale factor of 2, centre (0,0).

A'B' = 2 x AB	and	OA' = 2 x OA
A'C' = 2 x AC		OB' = 2 x OB
B'C' = 2 x BC		OC' = 2 x OC

Example

Triangle P'Q'R' is an enlargement of triangle PQR. What is the Scale Factor of the enlargement and the coordinates of the Centre of Enlargement?

To find the Centre of Enlargement:
Draw dotted lines passing through P and P' (-----), Q and Q' (-----), R and R' (-----). Where these dotted lines cross is the Centre of Enlargement. Coordinates are (0, 1).

To find the Scale Factor of the enlargement:
P'Q' = 10 units, PQ = 2 units, P'Q' = 5 x PQ. Scale Factor of the enlargement is 5.

Enlargement only changes the SIZE of the shape (i.e. the lengths of its sides) and its POSITION. Sometimes you are asked to calculate the Scale Factor and find the Centre of Enlargement. The Scale Factor of any enlargement is equal to the ratio of the lengths of any two corresponding sides in the object and the image.

Coordinates 1

Points on a Number Line

One coordinate is needed to identify a point on a number line i.e. in 1-D (in one dimension). On this number line, point A is (-2) and point B is (3).

Points in a Plane

Two coordinates are needed to identify a point in a plane i.e. in 2-D (in two dimensions). On the grid below point A is (3,4), B is (-2, 1) C is (-1, -4) and D is (1,-1).

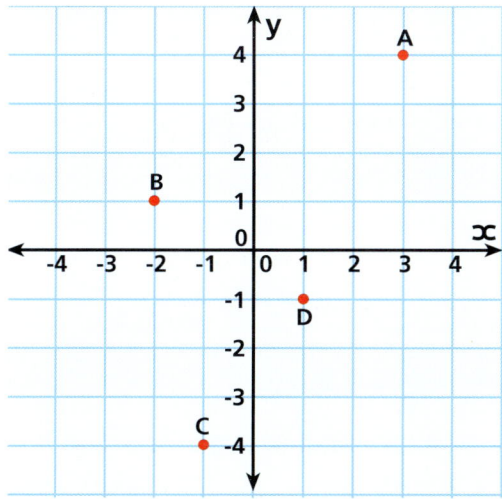

Coordinates can also be used to describe geometrical information. The coordinates of the following points: A is (3,2), B is (2, -2) C is (-3, -2) and D is (-2,2) are the vertices (corners) of a parallelogram.

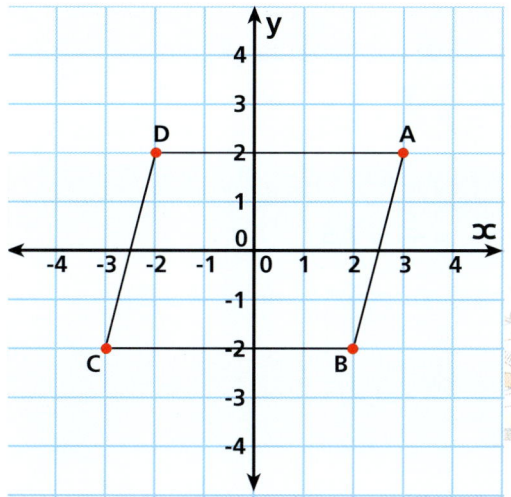

Points in Space

Three coordinates are needed to identify a point in space i.e. in 3-D (in three dimensions). Three axes each at right angles to each other are needed. The coordinates of each point represent distances from **0**, a fixed point, firstly parallel to the **x**-axis then parallel to the **y**-axis, and finally parallel to the **z**-axis.

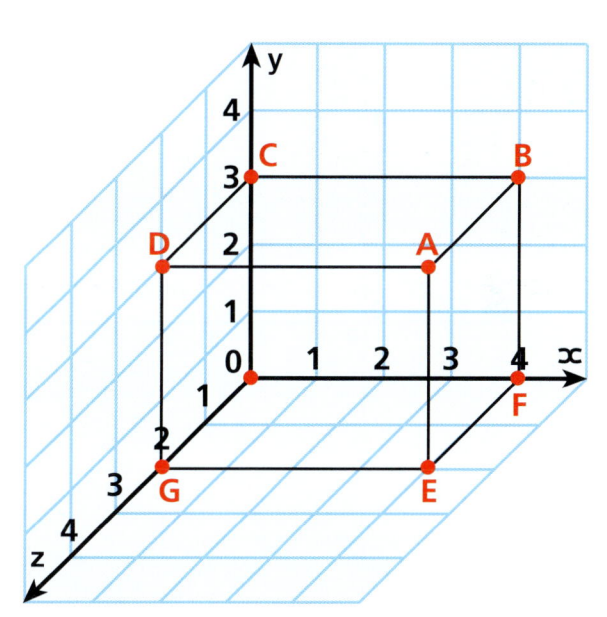

Point A is (4,3,2) since we need to go 4 units parallel to the **x**-axis, then 3 units parallel to the **y**-axis and finally 2 units parallel to the **z**-axis.

The other points would have the following coordinates: B is (4,3,0) C is (0,3,0) D is (0,3,2) E is (4,0,2) F is (4,0,0) and G is (0,0,2)

Picture courtesy of the AA

Coordinates 2

Coordinates of the Midpoint of a Line Segment

To find the coordinates of the midpoint, M, of a line segment AB you need to find ...
- the average of the x coordinates of points A and B. This is the x coordinate of the midpoint, M.
- the average of the y coordinates of points A and B. This is the y coordinate of the midpoint, M.

Examples ...

1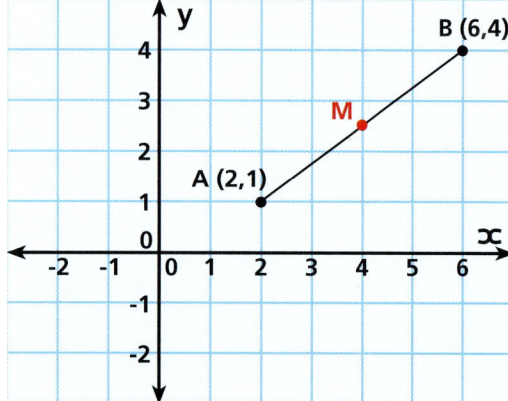

Average of x coordinates of points A and B
$= \dfrac{2+6}{2} = \dfrac{8}{2} = 4$

Average of y coordinates of points A and B
$= \dfrac{1+4}{2} = \dfrac{5}{2} = 2.5$

Coordinates of point M are (4, 2.5)

2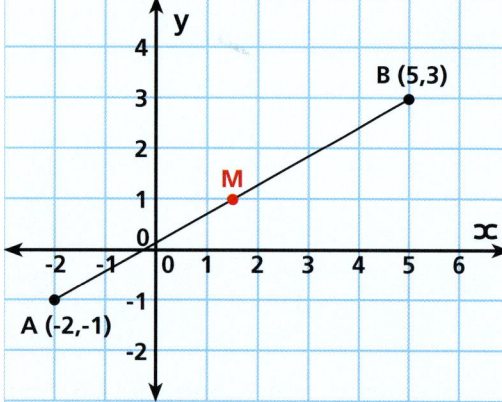

Average of x coordinates of points A and B
$= \dfrac{-2+5}{2} = \dfrac{3}{2} = 1.5$

Average of y coordinates of points A and B
$= \dfrac{-1+3}{2} = \dfrac{2}{2} = 1$

Coordinates of point M are (1.5, 1)

3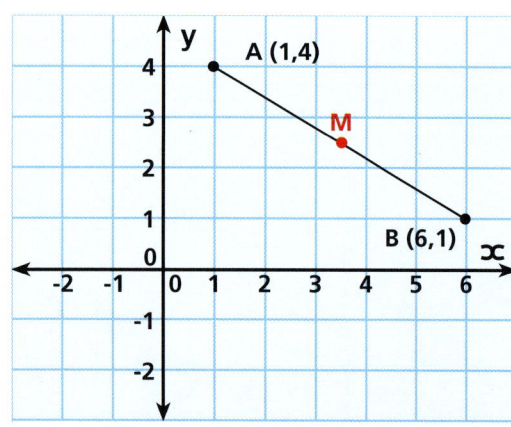

Average of x coordinates of points A and B
$= \dfrac{1+6}{2} = \dfrac{7}{2} = 3.5$

Average of y coordinates of points A and B
$= \dfrac{4+1}{2} = \dfrac{5}{2} = 2.5$

Coordinates of point M are (3.5, 2.5)

Perimeter 1

Perimeter

This is a measure of the distance all the way around the outside of a shape. All we need to know are the lengths of all the sides that make up the shape and then simply add them together.

Examples ...

The lengths of all the sides are given or can be worked out and so ...

Perimeter
= Length of AB + BC + CD + DE + EF + FA
= 6cm + 2.5cm + 4cm + (4.1-2.5)cm + 2cm + 4.1cm
= 20.2cm (remember the units)

The lengths of all the sides have to be measured using a ruler and so ...

Perimeter
= Length of AB + BC + CA
= 6.2cm + 5.7cm + 4.3cm
= 16.2cm (remember the units)

The lengths of all the sides can be found by counting squares and so ...

Perimeter
= Length of AB + BC + CD + DE + EF + FA
= 1cm + 3cm + 1cm + 1cm + 2cm + 4cm
= 12cm (remember the units)

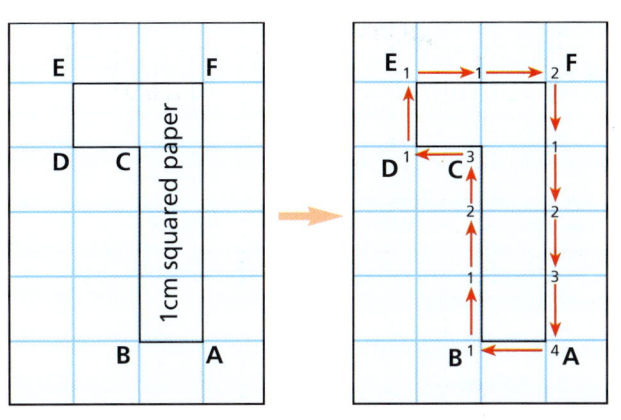

Perimeter 2

Circumference of a Circle

The circumference of a circle is a measure of the distance all the way around the outside of it. (Circumference is a mathematical word for the perimeter of a circle).

The **radius** is the distance from the centre, •, to the outside of the circle. The **diameter** is the distance from one side of the circle through the centre, •, to the other side of the circle which therefore means that:

Length of Radius = ½ x Length of Diameter
or Length of Diameter = 2 x Length of Radius

The circumference can be found by using this formula:

Circumference = 2πr or Circumference = πd

where π (called 'pi') has a value of 3.14 and 2πr means 2 x π x r and πd means π x d.

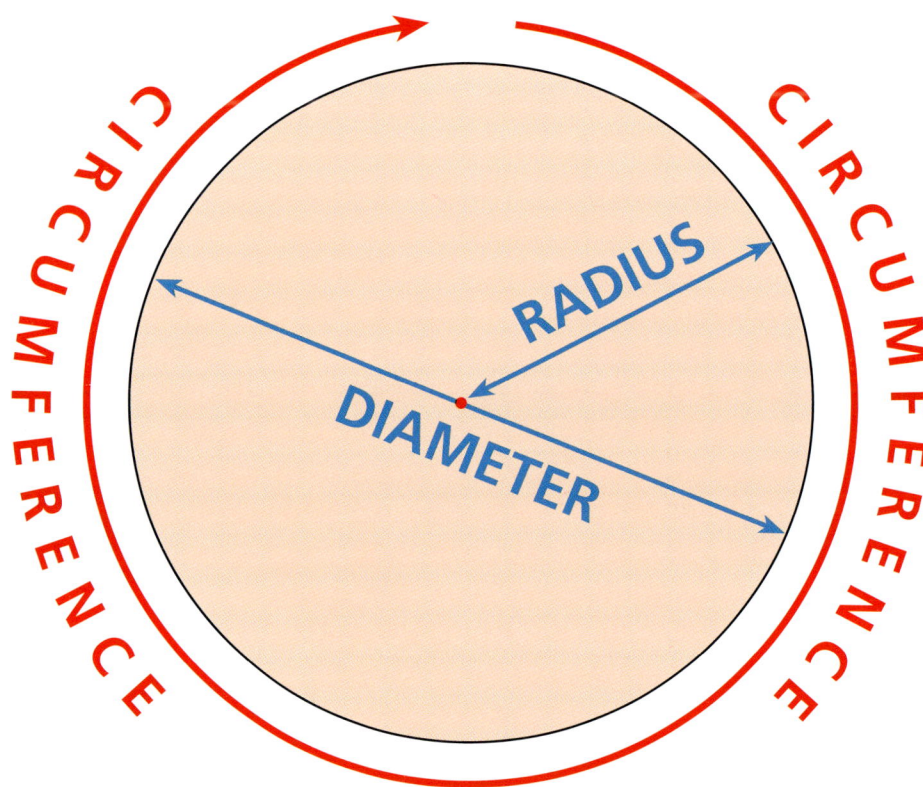

Examples ...

1 A circle has a radius of 2cm. Calculate its circumference.

Using our formula:
C = 2πr

We use this formula since we are given the RADIUS

C = 2 x π x 2cm
C = 2 x 3.14 x 2cm
C = **12.56cm** (remember the units)

2 A corn circle has a diameter of 20m. Calculate its circumference.

Using our formula:
C = πd

We use this formula since we are given the DIAMETER

C = π x 20m
C = 3.14 x 20m
C = **62.8m** (remember the units)

Area 1

Area

This is a measure of the amount of surface a two dimensional shape covers. Area is usually measured in **units²** e.g. **cm²** (cm squared) or **m²** (m squared) etc.

Estimation of Area Using Squared Paper

The area of a shape can be estimated if it has been drawn on squared paper. All we have to do is count the number of squares taken up by the shape.

This method is particularly useful when we have irregular shapes, although our answer will be an estimate of the area and not an exact value.

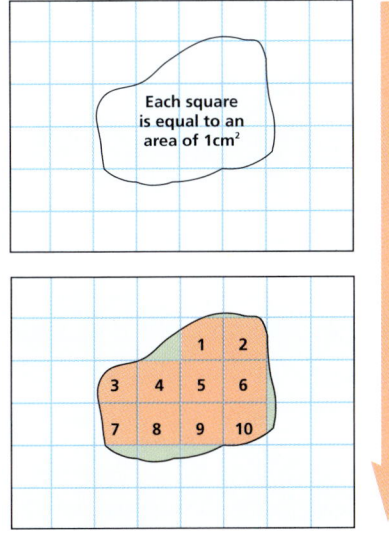

Count the whole squares and any squares more than half covered

Area = 10cm²

Areas of Common Shapes

The following shapes each have a formula which can be used to work out their area exactly.

Square

Rectangle

Parallelogram

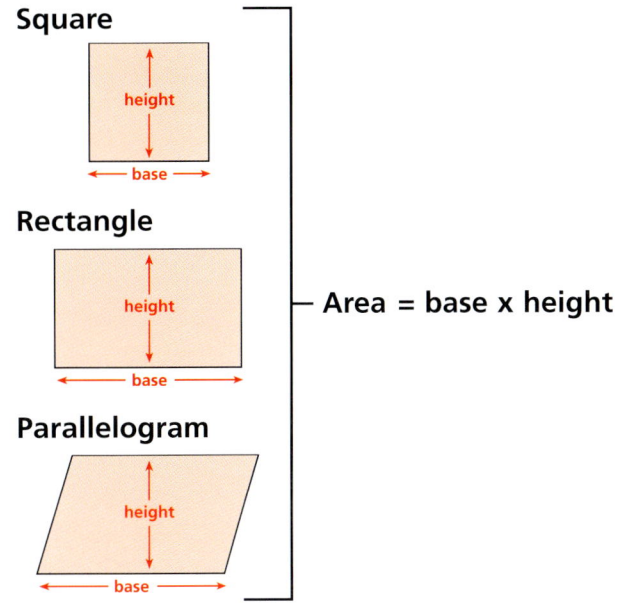

Area = base x height

Triangle

Area = $\frac{1}{2}$ x base x height

or ... = $\frac{\text{base x height}}{2}$

Trapezium

Area = $\frac{1}{2}$ (a + b) h

or ... = $\frac{(a + b)}{2}$ x h

Examples ...

1 Calculate the area of the following trapezium.

Using our formula: Area = $\frac{(a + b)}{2}$ x h

Area = $\frac{(10m + 6m)}{2}$ x 4m

= $\frac{16m}{2}$ x 4m

= 8m x 4m

= 32m² (remember the units)

2 The following parallelogram has an area of 24cm². Calculate its height if the length of its base is 10cm.

Using our formula: Area = Base x Height

24cm² = 10cm x Height

$\frac{24}{10}$ = $\frac{\cancel{10}}{\cancel{10}}$ x Height

Divide both sides by 10 to give us height on its own

Height = 2.4cm (remember the units)

Area 2

Deducing the Formula for the Area of a Parallelogram

The base of the parallelogram above is 4cm long and the perpendicular height is 2.5cm.

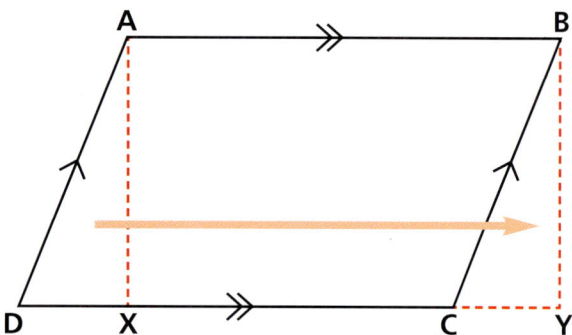

If we cut the triangle **ADX** off one side of the parallelogram and move it to the other side to form **BCY**, we create rectangle **ABYX** ...

... which has exactly the same area as our original parallelogram. Since ...

Area of a Rectangle = Base x Height
$$= 4 \times 2.5$$
$$= 10.0 \text{cm}^2$$

... this must also be the area of the parallelogram.

Area of a Parallelogram = Base x Height

Deducing the Formula for the Area of a Triangle

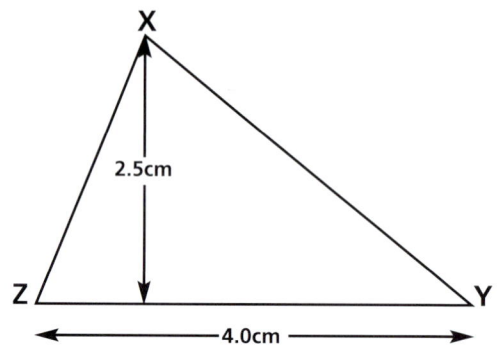

The base of the triangle above is 4cm long and the perpendicular height is 2.5cm.

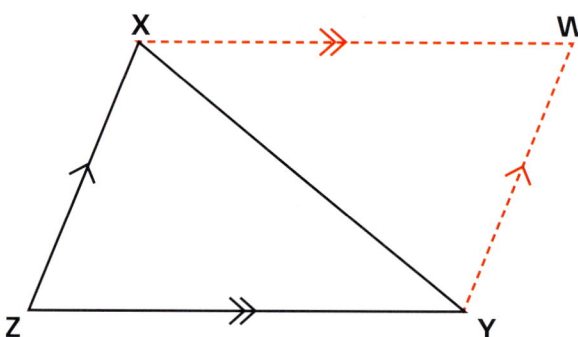

By drawing in the lines **XW** and **WY** we create a parallelogram. However the triangles **XYZ** and **XYW** are congruent (the same size and shape) ...

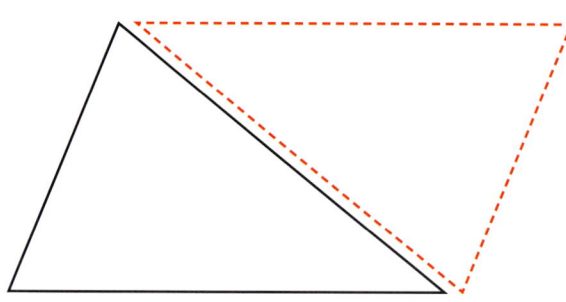

... which means that they have equal areas and are therefore exactly half of the area of the parallelogram.

Since the area of a parallelogram is equal to the base multiplied by the height, it follows that ...

Area of a Triangle = $\frac{1}{2}$ Base x Height
$$= \tfrac{1}{2} (4 \times 2.5)$$
$$= 5.0 \text{cm}^2$$

Area 3

Area of a Circle

The area of a circle is given by the formula:

Area = πr²

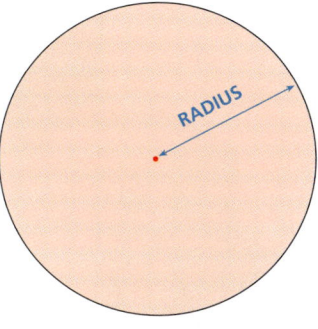

Yet again π has a value of **3.14** and πr² means **π x radius squared** or **π x r x r**. Don't get too worried about π (pi), it's just a different way of saying **3.14** ...

Example ...

A circular cricket field has a radius of 80m. Calculate its area (π = 3.14).

Using our formula:
$$\text{Area} = \pi r^2$$
$$= 3.14 \times 80^2$$
$$= 3.14 \times 6\,400$$
$$= 20\,096 m^2$$

Areas of Compound Shapes

These are shapes that can be divided up into smaller shapes. The area of each of these smaller shapes can then be calculated and added together.

Example ...

The diagram shows the layout for a side wall of a house. Calculate its area.

Area of 1 (Rectangle) = 9m x 8m = 72m²
Area of 2 (Square) = 3.5m x 3.5m = 12.25m²
Area of 3 (Triangle) = $\frac{9m \times 4m}{2}$ = 18m²
Area of wall = Area 1 + Area 2 + Area 3
$= 72m² + 12.25m² + 18m²$
$= 102.25m²$ (remember the units)

Surface Area of Solids

The surface area of any solid is simply the area of the NET which can be folded to completely cover the outside of the solid.

Examples ...

1 Calculate the surface area of the following triangular prism which has an equilateral triangle as its cross-section.

Area of 1 (Rectangle) = 10cm x 4cm = 40cm²
Therefore Area of 2 + 3 = 80cm²
Area of 4 (Triangle) = $\frac{4cm \times 3.5cm}{2}$ = 7cm²
Therefore Area of 5 = 7cm²

Surface Area of prism
= **Area of 1 + 2 + 3 + 4 + 5**
$= 40cm² + 80cm² + 7cm² + 7cm²$
$= 134cm²$ (remember the units)

2 Calculate the surface area of this cylinder.

Area of each end = πr²
$= 3.14 \times 1.5^2$
$= 7.065cm²$

Therefore both ends
$= 7.065 \times 2 = 14.13cm²$

Length of x = circumference of circle
$= 2\pi r$
$= 2 \times 3.14 \times 1.5$
$= 9.42cm$

Therefore area of rectangle
$= 7 \times 9.42$
$= 65.94cm²$

Therefore total area
$= 14.13cm² + 65.94cm²$
$= 80.07cm²$

Volume

Volume

This is a measure of the amount of space a 3-D object takes up. Volume is usually measured in **units³** e.g. **cm³** (cm cubed) or **m³** (m cubed) etc.

Calculation of the Volume of a Solid Made Up of Cubes

Providing we know the volume of one cube then all we have to do is work out how many cubes there are in each layer of the solid and then add them up.

Example

In the following example each cube has a volume of 1cm³.

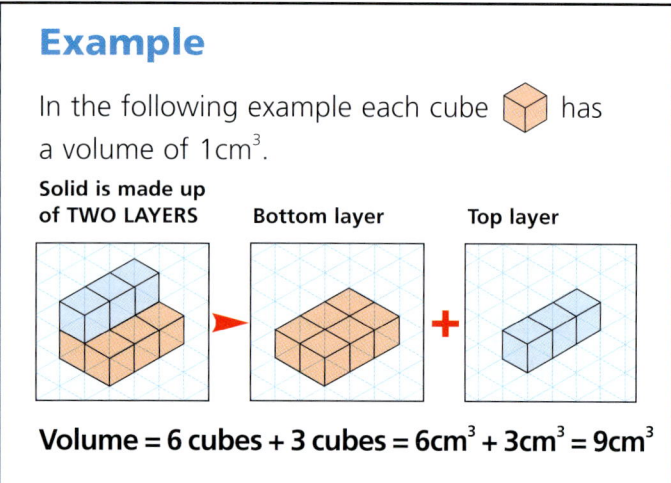

Volume = 6 cubes + 3 cubes = 6cm³ + 3cm³ = 9cm³

Volume of a Cuboid

The volume of a cuboid is given by the formula:

Volume
= length x width x height
= ℓ x w x h

Example

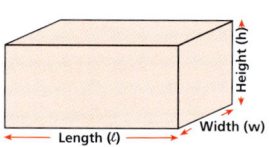

Using our formula:
Volume = length x width x height
= 6cm x 4cm x 2cm
= 48cm³ (remember the units)

Converting between cm³ and m³

Remember that **1cm³** =

whereas **1m³** =

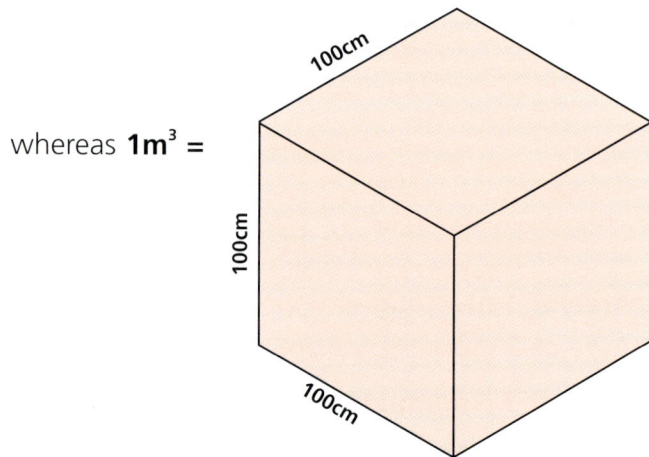

so **1m³** = 100cm x 100cm x 100cm
= 1 000 000cm³

3-D Shapes 1

Solids

A solid is a three-dimensional (3-D) shape. A very simple solid is the CUBE (a box with all its sides equal in length).

Here are some more examples of some common solids.

Types of Solid

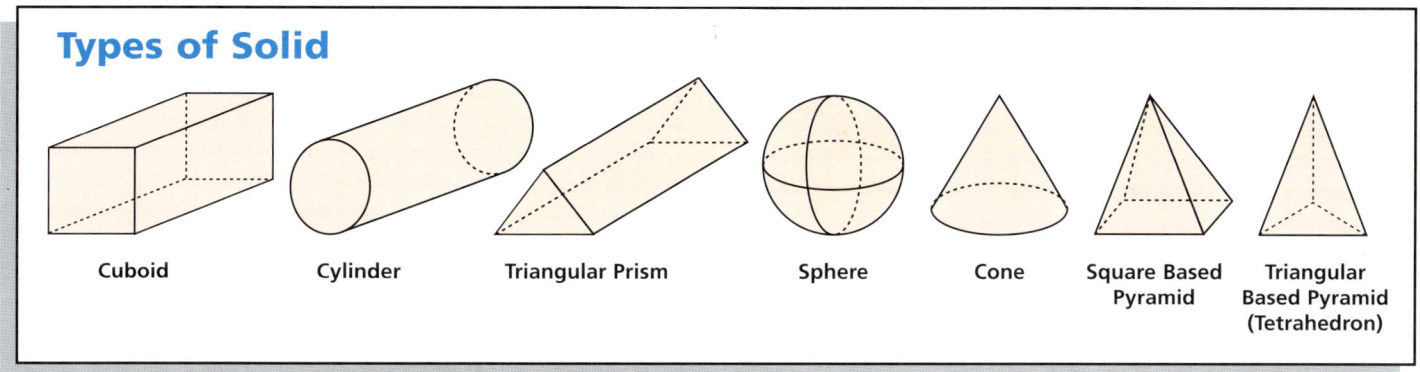

Cuboid   Cylinder   Triangular Prism   Sphere   Cone   Square Based Pyramid   Triangular Based Pyramid (Tetrahedron)

Drawing Solids Using Isometric Paper

A disadvantage of drawing solids like the ones above is that accurate measurements of all sides cannot be taken from the diagram. One way of drawing solids is to use isometric paper. This is a grid of equilateral triangles or dots. All solids can be drawn accurately and all measurements can be taken from the diagram.

Examples ...

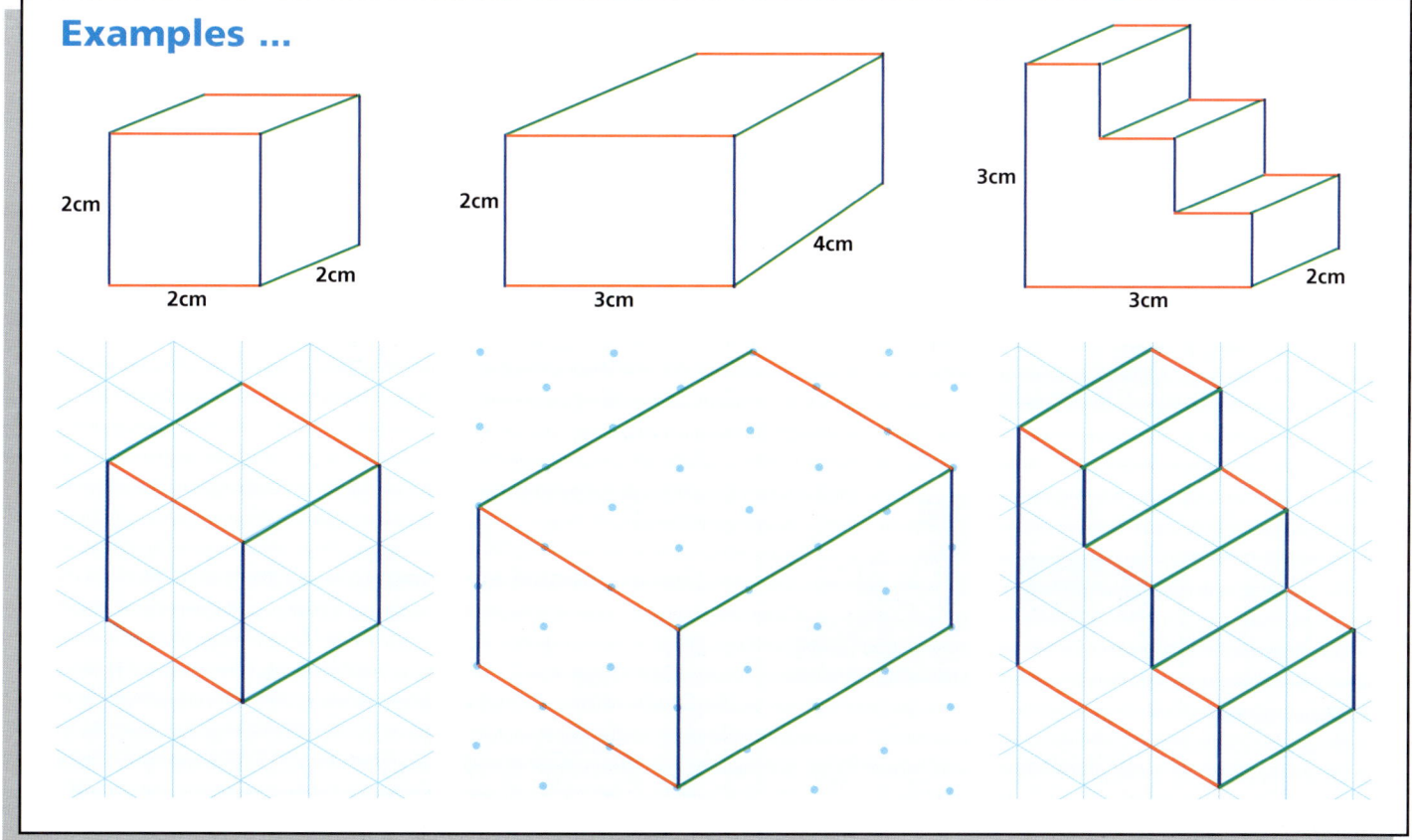

SHAPE, SPACE & MEASURES 65

3-D Shapes 2

Plans and Elevations

This is a picture of a car (a three-dimensional view of a solid). It is possible for us to have THREE different views of the car

- PLAN VIEW where we look down on the car from above
- FRONT ELEVATION where we look at the car from the front
- SIDE ELEVATION where we look at the car from the side

Example

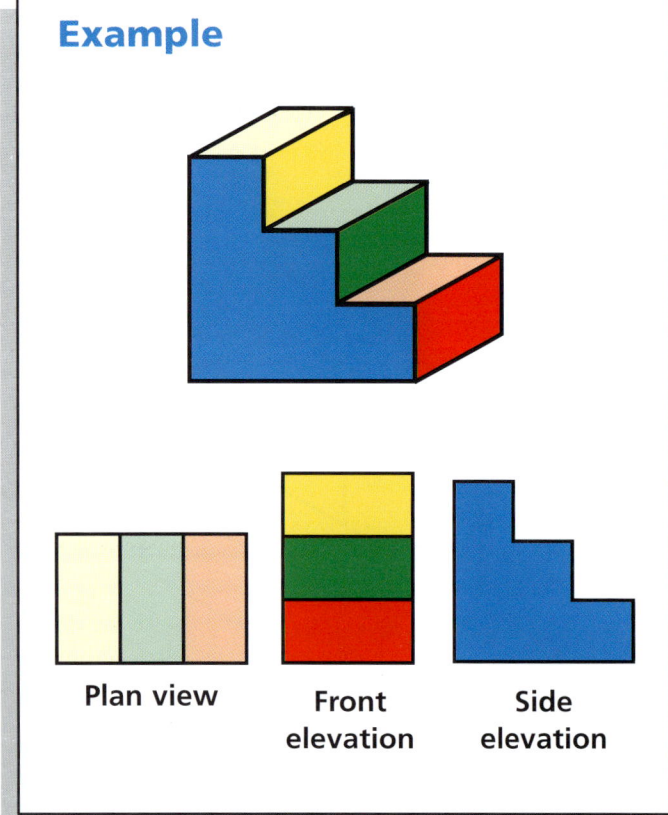

Nets for Solids

A net is a two-dimensional shape which can be folded to completely cover the outside of a solid.

Example

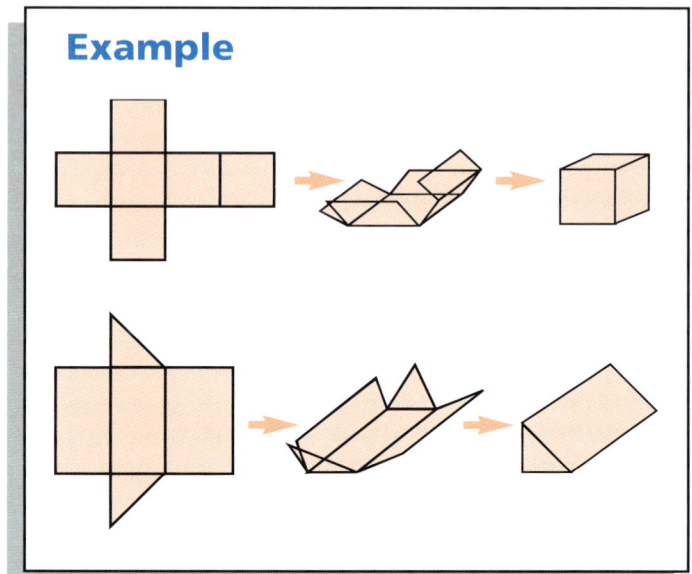

Plane Symmetry

A solid has plane symmetry if it can be 'cut in half' so that one half of the solid is an exact mirror image of the other half.

Examples ...

A cuboid has three planes of symmetry

A square based pyramid has four planes of symmetry

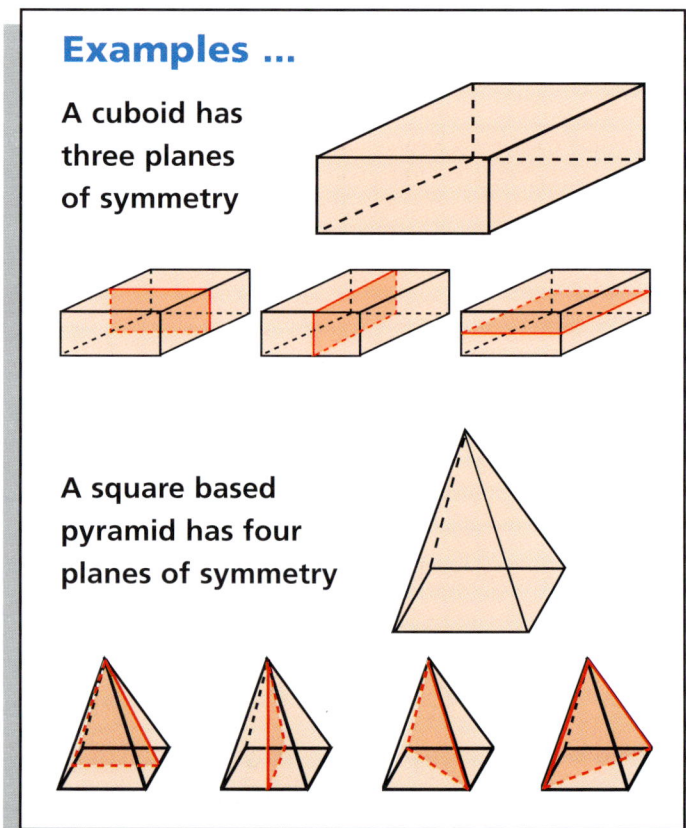

Symmetry 1

Line or Reflective Symmetry

A two-dimensional shape has a LINE OF SYMMETRY if it can be 'cut in half' so that one half of the shape is an exact mirror image of the other half of the shape.

The shapes opposite have 1 line of symmetry. These shapes can be 'cut in half' only once, and one half of the shape is congruent to the other half.

It is also possible for shapes to have more than 1 line of symmetry. These shapes (see below) can be 'cut in half' more than once.

A simple way to find lines of symmetry is to use tracing paper.

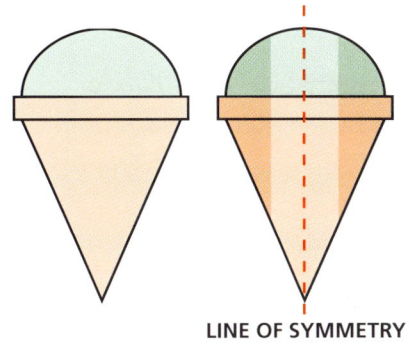

The left hand side of the dotted line is an exact mirror image of the right hand side and vice-versa

LINE OF SYMMETRY

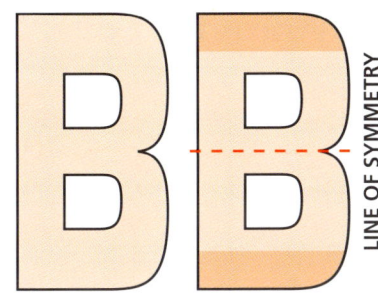

The top side of the dotted line is an exact mirror image of the bottom side and vice-versa

Two Lines of Symmetry

Draw in where you think the line of symmetry is and trace one side of your shape carefully on the tracing paper.

 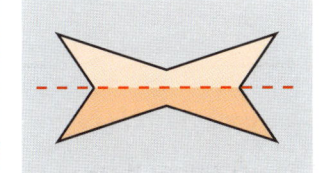

Flip the tracing paper over about the line of symmetry. If your line of symmetry is correct you should get an exact mirror image.

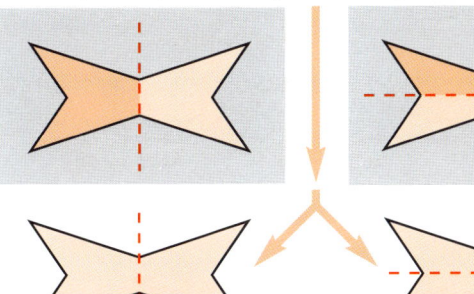

Three Lines of Symmetry

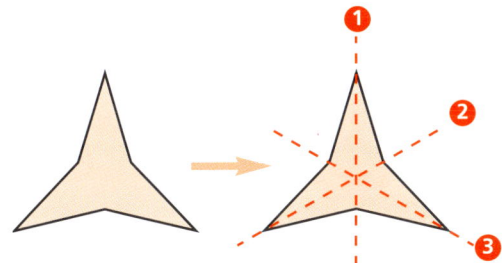

Four Lines of Symmetry

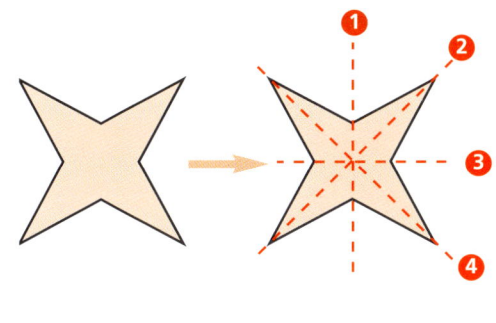

Some shapes, especially regular polygons (see p.50) can have even more lines of symmetry and there are shapes that have NO LINES OF SYMMETRY. These shapes cannot be 'cut in half' to give exact mirror images. Use tracing paper to check that the following shapes have no lines of symmetry.

Symmetry 2

Rotational Symmetry

A two-dimensional shape has ROTATIONAL SYMMETRY if it can be 'rotated about a point', called the Centre of Rotation, to a different position so that it looks the same as it was to begin with. The Order of Rotational Symmetry is equal to the number of times a shape fits onto itself in one 360° turn.

The following shape has ROTATIONAL SYMMETRY ORDER 2. This shape looks the same as its original position every time it is rotated half a turn (180°).

Rotational Symmetry Order 2

Original Position → → → Shape is now back to its original position

A simple way to investigate rotational symmetry is to use tracing paper.

Original Position — Draw in shape carefully on the tracing paper. Mark in Centre of Rotation. Place point of compass at X and rotate the paper.

Rotational Symmetry Order 3

Rotational Symmetry Order 4

Some shapes, especially regular polygons (see p.50) can have rotational symmetry of even higher orders and there are shapes that have ROTATIONAL SYMMETRY ORDER 1 (this can also be referred to as NO ROTATIONAL SYMMETRY). These shapes only look the same as their original position when they have been rotated one complete turn (360°)!!

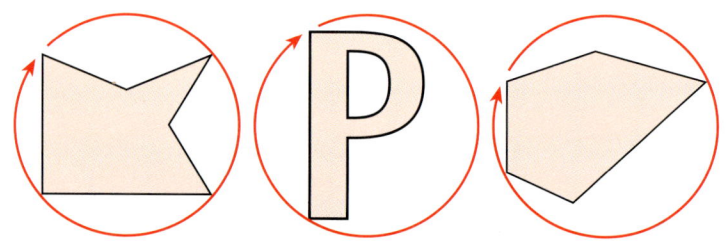

Scale Drawings & Map Scales

Drawing to Size and Scale

Before you attempt to construct any drawing to a particular size or scale you need the following:
- A PENCIL so any mistakes can be rubbed out without making a mess (and it looks a lot neater anyway).
- A RULER for the drawing of all straight lines.
- A PROTRACTOR for the measuring of any angles.
- A COMPASS for drawing circles, arcs and for any constructions.

Example

Here is a sketch map of an island. The map has four marker points A, B, C and D.

a) Make an accurate scale drawing of the quadrilateral ABCD using a scale of 1cm to represent 10km.

b) Calculate the length of BC.

a) Step 1: Draw the 90km line (9cm = 90km).
   Step 2: Measure and mark 80° and 90°.
   Step 3: Draw the 35km line (3.5cm = 35km) and the 45km line (4.5cm = 45km).
   Step 4: Complete the quadrilateral.

b) Length of BC = 8.4cm = 8.4 x 10km = 84km

Map Scales

This is part of a map of Devon and Cornwall which is drawn to a scale of 1cm : 10km

MAP DISTANCE in cm — Multiply (x) by 10 / 1cm : 10km / Divide (÷) by 10 — **ACTUAL DISTANCE in km**

A scale of 1cm : 10km means that a distance of 1cm measured on the map is an actual distance of 10km.

① The direct distance from Newquay to Plymouth as measured on the map is 7cm. Calculate the actual distance.

Actual dist = Map dist x 10

= 7 x 10 = 70km

② The actual direct distance between Torquay and Exeter is 30km. Calculate the map distance.

Map dist = Actual dist ÷ 10

= $\frac{30}{10}$ = 3cm

Measuring Bearings

Three-Figure Bearings

A bearing is a measurement of the position of one point relative to another point. It is measured in degrees. **Bearings are always measured from the north in a clockwise direction and are given as 3 digits**. Below are two points A and B. There are TWO possible bearings:

- The bearing of B from point A. This means that the measurement of the bearing is taken from point A.
- The bearing of A from point B. This means that the measurement of the bearing is taken from point B.

A circular protractor with a full 360° range can make three-figure bearings much easier to measure.

Sometimes the angle you measure from the N direction is less than 100° or even less than 10°. In this case one or two zeros are put in front of the angle in order to make them THREE-FIGURE BEARINGS.

Examples ...

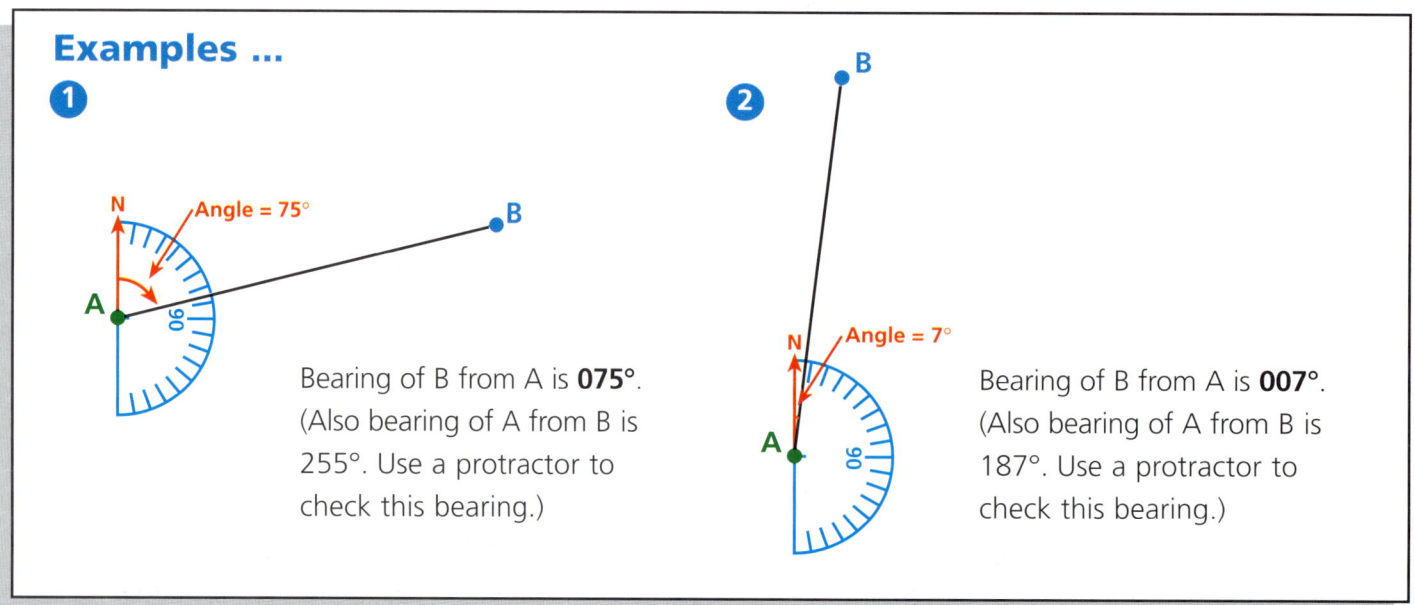

1 Bearing of B from A is **075°**. (Also bearing of A from B is 255°. Use a protractor to check this bearing.)

2 Bearing of B from A is **007°**. (Also bearing of A from B is 187°. Use a protractor to check this bearing.)

Reading Scales

Count Patterns

Most scales use simple count patterns based on the two, four, five or ten 'times' tables. They rely on the basic rules of decimals and fractions.

Once you have identified the count pattern you can take a reading on any straight, curved, horizontal or vertical scale.

Look at the different count patterns on these scales:

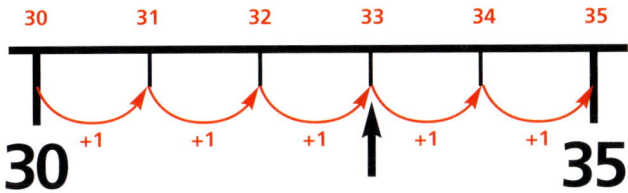

This scale goes up by one each time. In other words it has a count pattern of +1. So, the arrow gives a reading of 33.

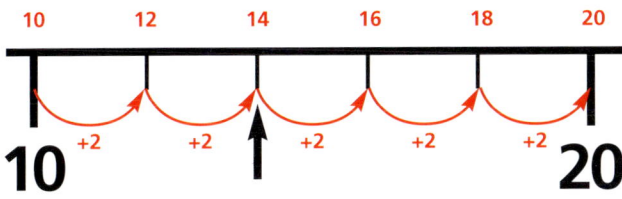

This scale goes up by two each time. In other words it has a count pattern of +2. The arrow gives a reading of 14.

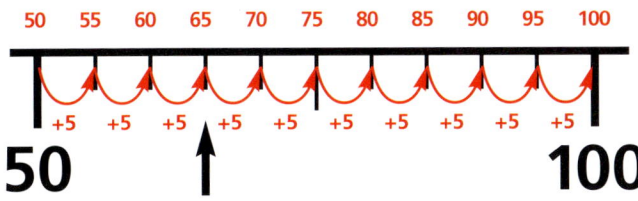

This scale goes up by five each time. In other words it has a count pattern of +5. The arrow gives a reading of 65.

This scale goes up by 0.1 (or $\frac{1}{10}$) each time. In other words it has a count pattern of +0.1. The arrow gives a reading of 1.5.

Examples ...

1 What is the reading on the thermometer?

- First you need to identify the count pattern. The numbers on the scale increase in tens. The lines in between have a count pattern of +1.
- Then you can take an accurate reading by counting up the scale from 20 (the last marked number) in ones.

20 + 4 = 24°

2 How much fruit juice has been collected in this measuring jug?

- Identify the count pattern. This time the numbers on the scale increase in fifties. The lines in between have a count pattern of +5.
- Take an accurate reading by counting up the scale from 50 (the last marked number) in fives.

50 + 45 = 95ml

3 A car tyre needs a pressure of 34psi. The pressure gauge shows the current pressure. How many more psi are needed in the tyre?

- Identify the count pattern. Again, the numbers on the scale increase in tens, but this time the lines in between have a count pattern of +2.
- Take an accurate reading by counting up the scale from 20 (the last marked number) in twos: 20 + 2 = 22psi.
- Now you can calculate the answer.

34 - 22 = 12psi needed.

You can check your answer by counting up the scale from 22 to 34.

Converting Measurements

Metric and Imperial Units

	Metric units	Approximate comparison between Metric & Imperial	Imperial units
Length	10mm = 1cm 100cm = 1m 1000m = 1km	2.5cm ≈ 1 inch 1m ≈ 39 inches 1600m ≈ 1 mile 8km ≈ 5 miles	12 inches = 1 foot 3 feet = 1 yard 1760 yards = 1 mile
Mass	1000mg = 1g 1000g = 1kg 1000kg = 1 tonne	30g ≈ 1 ounce 450g ≈ 1 pound 1kg ≈ 2.2 pounds	16 ounces = 1 pound 14 pounds = 1 stone
Capacity or Volume	1000ml = 1l 1000cm^3 = 1l (1ml = 1cm^3)	1l ≈ $1\frac{3}{4}$ pints 4.5l ≈ 1 gallon	8 pints = 1 gallon

Converting One Metric Unit to Another

Consider the conversion between centimetres (cm) and metres (m) as a typical example:

> Divide (÷) by 100 as we are going from a bigger number (100) to a smaller number (1)
>
> 100cm → 100cm = 1m → 1m
>
> Multiply (×) by 100 as we are going from a smaller number (1) to a bigger number (100)

Examples ...

1 Convert 300cm to metres.

From above: cm $\xrightarrow{\div 100}$ m

300cm = $\frac{300}{100}$ = 3m

2 Penny is 1.65m tall. What is her height in centimetres?

From above: m $\xrightarrow{\times 100}$ cm

1.65m = 1.65 × 100 = 165cm

Converting Between Metric and Imperial Units

These follow the same rules. Take the conversion between grams (g) and pounds.

> Divide (÷) by 450
>
> 450g → 450g ≈ 1 pound → 1 pound
>
> Multiply (×) by 450

Examples ...

1 A tin of baked beans has a mass of 600g. What is its mass in pounds?

From above: g $\xrightarrow{\div 450}$ pounds

600g = $\frac{600}{450}$ = 1.33 pounds (approx.)

2 A recipe for a cake needs 1.5 pounds of flour. What mass of flour is needed in grams?

From above: pounds $\xrightarrow{\times 450}$ g

1.5 pounds = 1.5 × 450 = 675g (approx.)

Speed

Speed

This is a measure of 'how fast' an object is moving. To calculate the speed of a moving object we need two measurements:

- the **DISTANCE** it moves and
- the **TIME** it takes to move that distance.

Speed can be calculated using the formula:

$$\text{Speed (S)} = \frac{\text{Distance (D)}}{\text{Time (T)}}$$

Speed is measured - in metres per second, m/s
- or kilometres per hour, km/h
- or miles per hour, mph

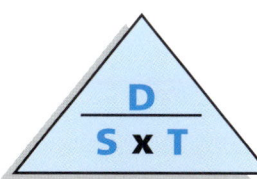

A FORMULA TRIANGLE makes it a lot easier for us when we want to calculate distance or time.

To get the formula for DISTANCE, cover 'D' up

DISTANCE = SPEED x TIME

To get the formula for TIME, cover 'T' up

$$\text{TIME} = \frac{\text{DISTANCE}}{\text{SPEED}}$$

Examples ...

1 Calculate the speed of a car which travels a distance of 90m in 10s.

$$\text{Speed} = \frac{90m}{10s} = 9\text{m/s} \text{ (remember the units)}$$

2 A train completes a journey of 150km at an average speed of 90km/h. How long did the journey take?

$$\text{Time} = \frac{\text{Distance}}{\text{Speed}} = \frac{150\text{km}}{90\text{km/h}}$$

$$= 1.\dot{6} = 1\frac{2}{3} = \textbf{1 hour 40 minutes}$$
(remember the units)

3 A car travels at 40km/h for 30 minutes and 80km/h for 15 minutes. How far does it travel in total?

Since given speeds are in km/h then times must be converted into hours before we do any calculations.

$$30 \text{ minutes} = \frac{30}{60} = 0.5 \text{ hours}$$

$$15 \text{ minutes} = \frac{15}{60} = 0.25 \text{ hours}$$

Distance = Speed x Time
a)   = 40 x 0.5 = 20km
b)   = 80 x 0.25 = 20km
Total Distance travelled = 40km

Constructions 1

Construction of Triangles

If you are given ...

... 3 sides: Construct the triangle ABC where AB = 3cm, BC = 2.5cm and AC = 2cm

| Draw AB of length 3cm | Draw arc from A of radius 2cm | Draw arc from B of radius 2.5cm | Complete the triangle |

... 2 sides & the included angle: Construct the triangle ABC where AB = 3cm, AC = 2cm and BÂC = 70°

| Draw AB of length 3cm | At A, measure and mark angle of 70° | Draw AC of length 2cm | Complete the triangle |

... 1 side & 2 angles: Construct the triangle ABC where AB = 3cm, BÂC = 50° and AB̂C = 30°

| Draw AB of length 3cm | At A, measure, mark and draw angle of 50° | At B, measure and mark angle of 30° | Complete the triangle |

For two triangles to be congruent they must both demonstrate one of the above set of conditions i.e. side, side, side (SSS); side, angle, side (SAS); angle, side, angle (ASA). In addition, right-angled triangles with a hypotenuse and side in common would also be congruent.

... 2 sides & the non-included angle: Construct the triangle ABC where AB = 3cm, AC = 2.3cm and AB̂C = 40°

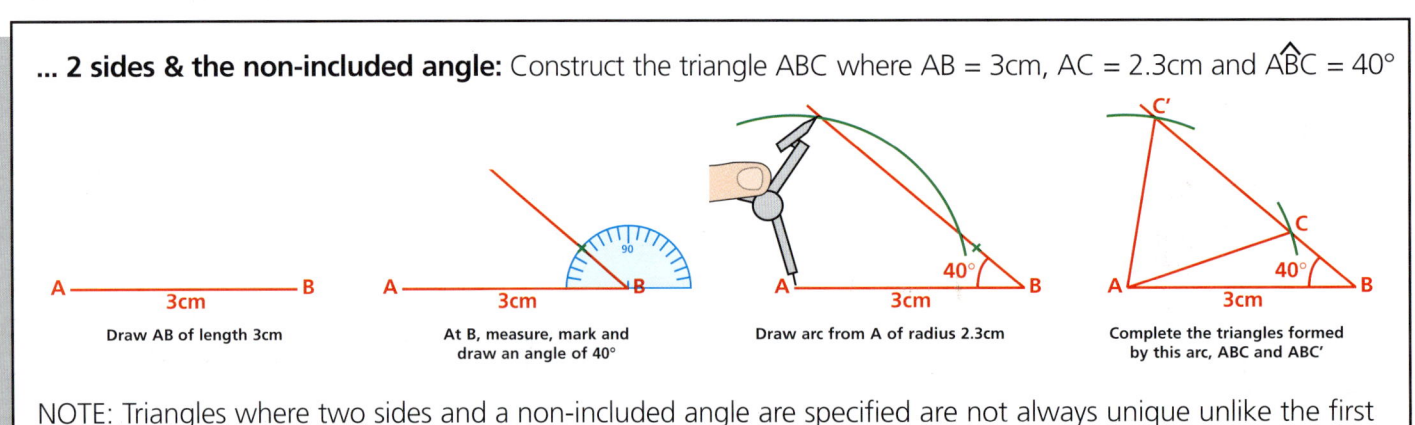

| Draw AB of length 3cm | At B, measure, mark and draw an angle of 40° | Draw arc from A of radius 2.3cm | Complete the triangles formed by this arc, ABC and ABC' |

NOTE: Triangles where two sides and a non-included angle are specified are not always unique unlike the first three examples above. This is simply due to the fact that the arc from A can cut the opposite side twice.

Constructions 2

Construction of a Regular Hexagon inside a Circle.

A simple way to do this is as follows:

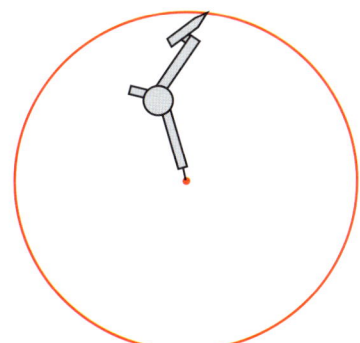

First of all construct the circle with the radius you require.

Using the same radius, place the compass point anywhere on the circumference and draw an arc.

Using the same radius again, place the compass on the point where the arc intersects the circumference and draw another arc.

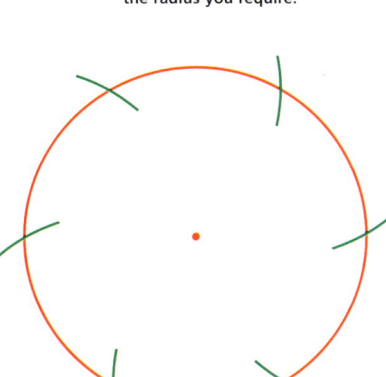

Repeat this process until you have six equal arcs on the circumference of the circle. The final arc should intersect the circumference at your starting point.

Use a ruler to draw a straight line between the first two points where the arcs intersect the circumference of the circle.

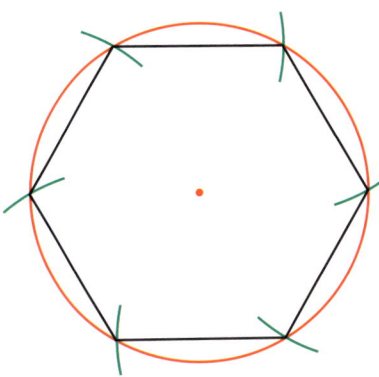

Repeat this process, joining up all the points to form a regular hexagon.

Properties of Circles

The following six diagrams relate to terms used to describe various properties of circles. You need to be completely familiar with all of these.

The **CENTRE** of the circle is the only point which is the same distance from every point on the circumference. The **CIRCUMFERENCE** is the line which defines the edge of the circle.

The **RADIUS** is formed by any straight line drawn from the centre of the circle to the circumference. It is always half the diameter of the circle.

The **DIAMETER** is a straight line which passes through the centre of the circle to join opposite points on the circumference.

A **CHORD** is a straight line joining two points on the circumference which DOES NOT pass through the centre of the circle.

A **TANGENT** is a straight line which touches the circumference of a circle.

An **ARC** is simply part of the circumference of a circle.

Probability

The Nature of Probability

Probability, quite simply is a measure of the likelihood of a particular event occurring. Probability is used throughout the world in order to give a sound mathematical basis for predicting future events. These events can be relatively simple such as tossing a coin or spinning a roulette wheel, however they can also be vastly complicated such as in the assessment of large insurance risk.

Probability Scale and the Language of Probability

For an event to happen we might say that its probability is 'a certainty', 'more than likely', 'evens' or '50/50', 'not very likely', 'no chance'. The probability of an event occurring (or not occurring) can be stated as either a fraction, percentage or decimal. These can be shown on a probability scale. Here is a very simple one:

These are the only probabilities you can have i.e. you cannot have a probability greater than 1.
Thus if the probability of something happening is P, then the probability of it not happening is 1 - P

0	$\frac{1}{10}$	$\frac{2}{10}$	$\frac{3}{10}$	$\frac{4}{10}$	$\frac{5}{10}$	$\frac{6}{10}$	$\frac{7}{10}$	$\frac{8}{10}$	$\frac{9}{10}$	1
0	10%	20%	30%	40%	50%	60%	70%	80%	90%	100%
0	0.1	0.2	0.3	0.4	0.5	0.6	0.7	0.8	0.9	1
No chance i.e. impossible			Not very likely		Evens 50/50			More than likely		A certainty i.e. bound to happen

Examples ...

1 The probability of you passing a maths test is $\frac{7}{10}$. What is the probability that you will fail?

Since you can only pass or fail, the total probability = 1. Therefore ...

P(passing) + P(failing) = 1
$\quad$ P(failing) = 1 - P(passing)
$\qquad\qquad = 1 - \frac{7}{10}$
$\qquad\qquad = \frac{3}{10}$

...which means that you are not very likely to fail!

2 A drawer contains white, black and red socks only. If the probability of picking a white sock at random is 0.2 and a black sock is 0.3, what is the probability of picking a red sock?

Since the drawer only contains white, black and red socks, the total probability = 1. Therefore ...

P(w) + P(b) + P(r) = 1
$\quad$ P(r) = 1 - (P(w) + P(b))
$\qquad = 1 - (0.2 + 0.3)$
$\qquad = 1 - 0.5$
$\qquad = 0.5$

...which means that you have an even chance of picking a red sock at random.

Mutually Exclusive Outcomes

When one outcome prevents another outcome from taking place, the two outcomes are said to be MUTUALLY EXCLUSIVE. This can also be the case when there are three or more possible outcomes.

Outcomes with Equal Chances

The important rule to remember is this: 'If there are '**n**' mutually exclusive outcomes, all of which are equally likely, then the probability of one outcome happening is $\frac{1}{n}$'.

Examples ...

1. **Tossing a coin:** Here there are two mutually exclusive outcomes, Heads or Tails - if you throw a Head you can't throw a Tail!

   P(Heads) = $\frac{1}{2}$
   P(Tails) = $\frac{1}{2}$

   Note that the probability of each outcome added together is 1. i.e. $\frac{1}{2} + \frac{1}{2} = 1$

2. **Spinning a Spinner:** Here there are three mutually exclusive outcomes since if you spin a red, you can't spin any other colour!

   P(Red) = $\frac{1}{3}$
   P(Blue) = $\frac{1}{3}$
   P(Green) = $\frac{1}{3}$

   Note that the probability of each outcome added together is 1. i.e. $\frac{1}{3} + \frac{1}{3} + \frac{1}{3} = 1$

3. **Throwing a die:** Here are six mutually exclusive outcomes, since throwing any one number prevents you from throwing the rest.

   P(one) = $\frac{1}{6}$
   P(two) = $\frac{1}{6}$
   P(three) = $\frac{1}{6}$
   P(four) = $\frac{1}{6}$
   P(five) = $\frac{1}{6}$
   P(six) = $\frac{1}{6}$

   Note that the probability of each outcome added together is 1. i.e. $\frac{1}{6} + \frac{1}{6} + \frac{1}{6} + \frac{1}{6} + \frac{1}{6} + \frac{1}{6} = 1$

Outcomes with Unequal Chances

The important rule to remember is this: 'If there are '**n**' mutually exclusive outcomes, but only '**a**' desired outcomes, then the probability of a desired outcome is $\frac{a}{n}$'.

Examples ...

1. **Picking a Ball (from inside a bag):** With this set of balls there are four mutually exclusive outcomes - black, green, yellow and orange. However, the chances of each colour being picked are not equal, since there are 5 blacks, 4 greens, 2 yellows and 1 orange.

   P(black) = $\frac{5}{12}$
   P(green) = $\frac{4}{12}$ or $\frac{1}{3}$
   P(yellow) = $\frac{2}{12}$ or $\frac{1}{6}$
   P(orange) = $\frac{1}{12}$

   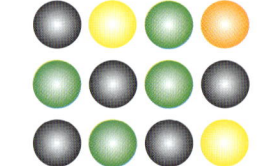

   Note that the probability of each outcome added together is 1 i.e. $\frac{5}{12} + \frac{1}{3} + \frac{1}{6} + \frac{1}{12} = 1$

2. **Spinning a Spinner:** With this spinner there are three mutually exclusive outcomes - red, blue and green. Since the spinner has 3 reds, 2 blues and 1 green, there is an unequal chance of getting each colour.

   P(red) = $\frac{3}{6}$ or $\frac{1}{2}$
   P(blue) = $\frac{2}{6}$ or $\frac{1}{3}$
   P(Green) = $\frac{1}{6}$

   Note that the probability of each outcome added together is 1 i.e. $\frac{1}{2} + \frac{1}{3} + \frac{1}{6} = 1$

Listing all Outcomes

Outcomes of Single Events

1. **Tossing a coin.** Here there are only two outcomes: Heads or Tails
2. **Spinning a three sided spinner.** Here there are three outcomes: Red, Blue or Green
3. **Throwing a die.** Here there are only six outcomes: One, Two, Three, Four, Five or Six

In all cases like these all you have to do is make a simple list.

Outcomes of Two Successive Events

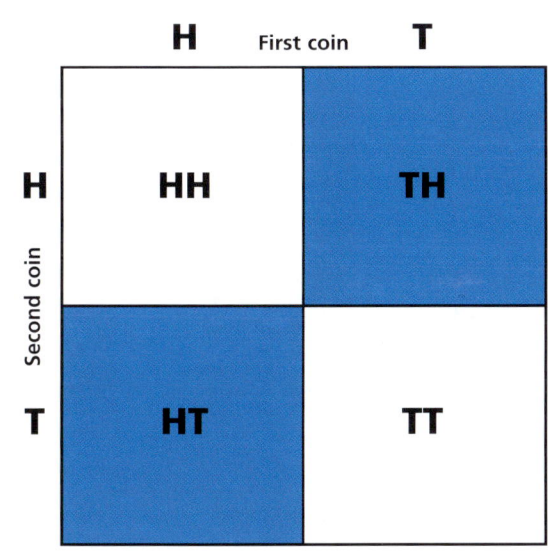

1. **Tossing two coins, one after the other.**
   In cases like these it is easier to use a sample space diagram to show the possible outcomes. With two coins there are 4 outcomes. The chances of each are:

   P(Head + Head) = $\frac{1}{4}$
   P(Tail + Tail) = $\frac{1}{4}$
   P(Head + Tail) = $\frac{1}{4}$
   P(Tail + Head) = $\frac{1}{4}$

   Note that once again the probability of each outcome added together is 1.
   i.e. $\frac{1}{4} + \frac{1}{4} + \frac{1}{4} + \frac{1}{4} = 1$

2. **Throwing a pair of die.**
   In this case, each die has six possible outcomes. The sample space diagram, which shows the scores of the two dice added together, reveals a total of 36 possible outcomes. Each outcome (e.g. throwing a 4 with the first die and a 2 with the second) has a $\frac{1}{36}$ probability.

   However, while there is only a $\frac{1}{36}$ chance of scoring a total of either 2 or 12, there is a $\frac{6}{36}$ or $\frac{1}{6}$ chance of scoring a seven.

Estimated Probability

Theoretical Probability

Since the chance of a coin landing on Heads is $\frac{1}{2}$, then the number of Heads we should expect in 10 tosses is:

$\frac{1}{2} \times 10 = 5$.

This however is not always the case in reality ...

Estimated Probability

A simple experiment was carried out where a coin was tossed 10, 100 and a 1 000 times. The graphs opposite show the number of Heads and Tails obtained. In our experiment we would expect to always get the same number of Heads and Tails as the probability of each event occurring is $\frac{1}{2}$ or 0.5.

A theoretical estimate of the number of heads we should obtain is given by the probability multiplied by the number of times the coin is tossed.
i.e. 0.5 x 1000 = 500

Alternatively, an estimated probability can be obtained by experiment. Simply tossing the coin enough times can give us a good indication.

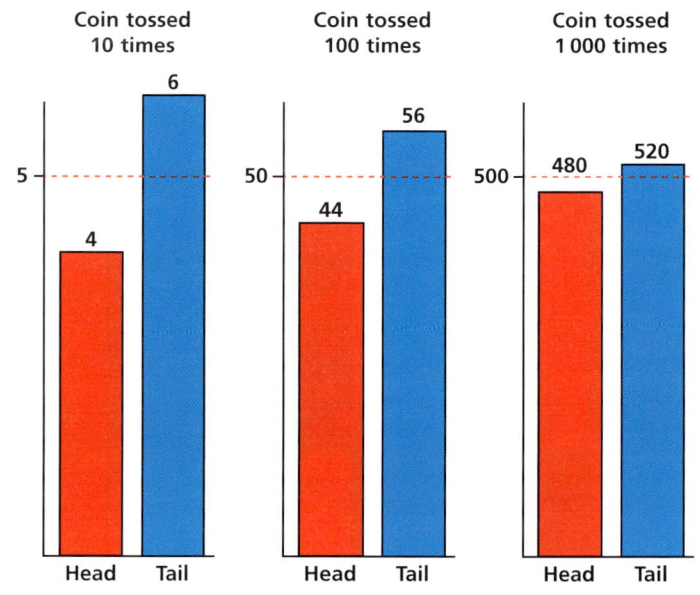

Estimated Probability =

$$\frac{\text{Number of Heads (or Tails) we get}}{\text{Total number of times the coin was tossed}}$$

	Coin tossed 10 times	Coin tossed 100 times	Coin tossed 1 000 times
Head	Head = $\frac{4}{10}$ = 0.4	Head = $\frac{44}{100}$ = 0.44	Head = $\frac{480}{1000}$ = 0.48
Tail	Tail = $\frac{6}{10}$ = 0.6	Tail = $\frac{56}{100}$ = 0.56	Tail = $\frac{520}{1000}$ = 0.52

Importance of Sample Size

As you can see from the data above, the bigger the sample, the more reliable it is. It would be easy to believe that tossing a coin ten times could produce 2 tails and 8 heads!

This has implications in testing for bias. For instance it would be possible to test experimentally the frequency of red and black on a roulette wheel. If there was time to take a big enough sample then it would be possible to say with some justification that the wheel wasn't fair, e.g. if 50 000 spins produce 26 750 reds and 23 250 blacks!!

Collecting Data 1

Some Definitions

- **Primary Data:** is data which has been directly obtained first hand, either by yourself or by someone under your direction. It can be collected by questionnaire, survey, observation, experiment or data logging.

- **Secondary Data:** is data which has been obtained independently by an external agency and which may be already stored either in printed or electronic form e.g. published statistics, data from the internet.

- **The Population:** is the total number of items you are investigating.

- **The Sample:** is the limited number of items that you have selected to represent the whole population.

- **A Random Sample:** is a sample in which every item of the population has an equal chance of being selected.

Reasons for Sampling

Information is a hugely powerful tool in modern society but clearly it is impossible to survey huge populations. Sampling allows us to look at a cross-section of the population, making the process much quicker and much cheaper! Samples are used widely to inform opinion polls, market research, to produce T.V. viewing figures and to provide trend analysis.

Identifying Bias in Samples

Consider the following dodgy examples of sampling:

- A recent survey suggests that 82% of the population prefer Rugby League to Soccer. The survey was conducted in St Helens.

- A High Street survey reveals that 76% of men aged between 18 and 42 go to the pub at least once a week. The survey was conducted at 11pm.

- A telephone survey suggests that 100% of the population has at least one telephone in their house.

In order to be unbiased, every individual in the population must have an equal chance of being included in the sample. This means taking into account:

- The time of day of the survey
- The age range
- Relative affluence
- The geographical area
- Ethnicity
- Lifestyle

However, you must also remember that THE BIGGER THE SAMPLE SIZE, THE MORE REPRESENTATIVE IT'S LIKELY TO BE (assuming of course that you have minimised all the other potential areas of bias).

Collecting Data 2

Collecting Data by Observation

This can be laborious and time consuming but for some things it is the best way. For instance a traffic survey might be done in this way to reveal the volume of traffic using a bridge. You must remember to ask yourself whether the survey is being conducted at and for an appropriate time.

Collecting Data by Experiment

People involved in the Sciences use experiments to gather data to support their hypotheses. The key things to remember are that the experiment must be repeated an appropriate number of times, and also that the experiment must be capable of being repeated by someone else.

Collecting Data by Questionnaire

Questionnaires are skillfully designed forms which are used to conduct surveys of a sample of the population.

Designing a Questionnaire

Good questionnaires have the following things in common …

- They are not too long. Never more than 10 questions, but less if possible.
- They contain questions which are easily understood and do not cause confusion.
- They ask for simple, short answers, e.g. Yes/No, Like/Don't Like or Male/Female
- They avoid vague words like Tall, Old, Fast, Good etc.
- The questions do not show any bias, e.g. 'Do you agree that rugby is a more watchable game than hockey?'
- They only contain relevant questions.

Example

Yasmin decides to test the hypothesis that 'Parents would prefer the school holidays to be shorter' by using the following questionnaire.

QUESTIONNAIRE

1. Do you have children of school age?
   Yes ❏ No ❏
   — *This tests whether the questionnaire is relevant to this person*

2. How many children do you have?
   1 ❏ 2 ❏ 3 ❏ 4+ ❏
   — *The answer may be affected by the size of the family!*

3. To which age group do they belong?
   11-13 ❏ 14-16 ❏ 17-18 ❏
   — *The answer may turn out to be dependent upon the age of the person's children!*

4. Are you in full time employment?
   Yes ❏ No ❏
   — *This tells us whether or not the person will see a lot of his/her children over the holidays!*

5. Do you think the school holidays are…
   Too Short? ❏
   Too Long? ❏
   Just Right? ❏
   — *This avoids asking a 'loaded question' i.e. it avoids bias*

From the answers, Yasmin could …

1. Reject any responses from people who aren't parents.
2. Analyse the data to see if family size, age range and employment status affect the answers.
3. Come up with a pretty good answer to her original hypothesis.

Sorting Data 1

Data comes in many different forms. To make sense of the data it is often sorted and collated together. There are two different types of data that you can record for sorting and collating.

Discrete and Continuous Data

Discrete data is data that can only have certain values. For example, the number of goals a football team can score in a match is 0, 1, 2, 3, 4 etc. They cannot have a score in between, like 0.5, 1.6, 2.2 etc.

Continuous data is data that can have any value. It tends to be obtained by reading measuring instruments. The accuracy of the data is dependent on the precision of the equipment.

Tally Charts and Frequency Tables

Very often the best way to sort and collate discrete or continuous data is to draw a tally chart and a frequency table.

Example

Here are the results of the games involving England, France, Croatia and Switzerland in their group games from the 2004 European Championships. Sort the number of goals scored per game by each team by drawing a tally chart and a frequency table.

Since the range of data here is narrow (e.g. from 0 to 4 goals scored) each value can be included individually in the tally chart and frequency table. As you complete the tally column always tick off each number as you go along. This makes sure that you don't include the same number twice or miss any out.

The numbers in the frequency column are simply the number of tallies. Remember to add them up, as this total is equal to the total number of pieces of data (not, in this example, the total number of goals scored!).

The data in this example is discrete, however, the same process would apply for continuous data.

Switzerland 0 Croatia 0	France 2 England 1
England 3 Switzerland 0	Croatia 2 France 2
Croatia 2 England 4	Switzerland 1 France 3

Number of goals scored	Tally	Frequency of that no. of goals being scored by a team
0	|||	3
1	||	2
2	||||	4
3	||	2
4	|	1

TOTAL = 12

HANDLING DATA 83

Sorting Data 2

Using Class Intervals

Sometimes, unlike the example on the previous page, the data is so widespread that it is impractical to include each value in the tally chart and frequency table individually. When this happens, the data is sorted into groups called class intervals, where each class interval represents a range of values.

Example

The newspaper cutting shows the recorded temperatures in °C for various places both at home and abroad. Sort the recorded temperatures by drawing a tally chart and a frequency table.

Temperatures home and abroad

Amsterdam	19	Cairo	34	Majorca	27	New York	32
Athens	33	Cardiff	16	Manchester	12	Newcastle	13
Barbados	29	Dublin	15	Miami	26	Paris	20
Barcelona	26	Jersey	20	Milan	28	Peking	33
Berlin	23	London	21	Montreal	22	Prague	26
Bermuda	28	Madrid	33	Moscow	15	Rhodes	28

As you can see, the data here is widespread e.g. from 12°C to 34°C. Out of practicality, the temperature values are arranged in groups of five in our tally chart and frequency table.

The class interval $10 \leqslant T < 15$ would include any temperature reading equal to or greater than 10°C and less than 15°C (a temperature reading of 15°C is included in the next class interval) and so on. Remember to total the numbers in the frequency column to make sure they add up to the total number of locations (pieces of data).

Recorded temperatures, T(°C)	Tally	Frequency of temperatures falling within that range
$10 \leqslant T < 15$	||	2
$15 \leqslant T < 20$	||||	4
$20 \leqslant T < 25$	⧻	5
$25 \leqslant T < 30$	⧻ |||	8
$30 \leqslant T < 35$	⧻	5
		TOTAL = 24

The data in this example is continuous, however, the same process would apply for discrete data.

Two Important Points

- The format of class intervals can vary. The following class intervals could have been used to give the same results for the data above: 10-14, 15-19, 20-24 etc.
- The range of each class interval depends on the total range of the data. If the total range of the data is large and the range of each class interval is small, then your frequency table would have a lot of rows. Aim to have no more than 10 lines in your table!

Sorting Data 3

Stem and Leaf Diagrams

A stem and leaf diagram sorts data into groups. An advantage over frequency tables is that they enable you to get more of a feel for the 'shape' of distribution. For example, the following data shows the length of time (in minutes) it took 30 pupils to complete a test, arranged in ascending order:

8, 8, 9, 15, 15, 16, 16, 17, 18, 18, 20, 21, 21, 22, 23, 26, 27, 27, 28, 28, 29, 33, 34, 34, 35, 39, 39, 42, 48, 49.

This data can be represented using a stem and leaf diagram by taking the tens to form the 'stem' of the diagram and the units to form the 'leaves'.

The end product is similar to a frequency table. However, besides allowing you to visualise the 'shape' of the data, it can be used to identify the modal class i.e. the 20-29 group and the median i.e. 24.5 (between the 15th and 16th piece of data as there are 30 values).

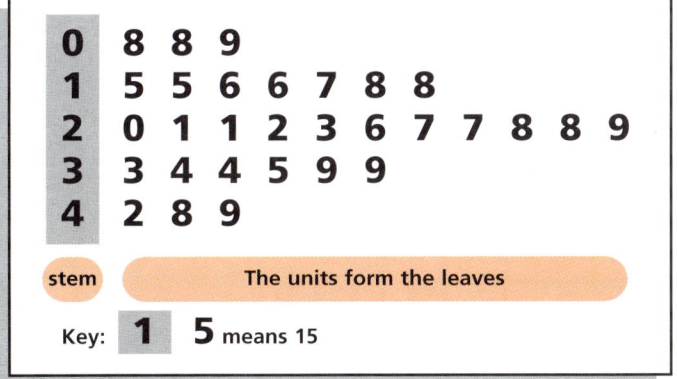

Two Way Tables

These simply show two sets of information, one vertically and the other horizontally. Information organised in this way can actually result in you gaining more information than you started with.

For instance: 'In a survey, 200 Year 7 and 8 pupils were asked if they preferred Maths or Science. 73 out of 110 year 7 pupils preferred Maths, and in total 82 pupils preferred Science.' This could lead to the table below:

	YEAR 7	YEAR 8	TOTAL
SCIENCE			82
MATHS	73		
TOTAL	110		200

… which in turn can be used to work out the missing data:

	YEAR 7	YEAR 8	TOTAL
SCIENCE	37	45	82
MATHS	73	45	118
TOTAL	110	90	200

Notice that in the original table there was no data for Year 8 … now it's all there!

Various Types of Table

Tables can be arranged in many different ways to suit the purpose for which they are intended. Remember, the idea is to make the information as accessible as possible, so you've got to give a bit of thought as to how you want to present it.

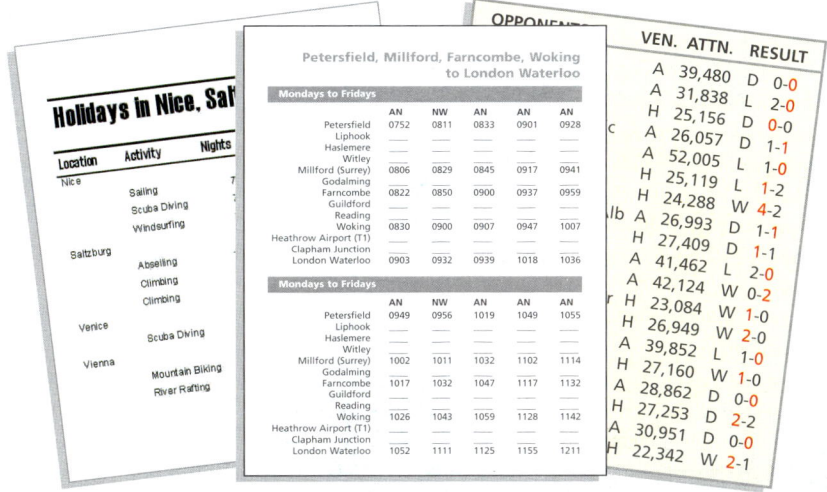

Lonsdale REVISION GUIDES

HANDLING DATA

Displaying Data 1

The best way of displaying data that has been sorted into a frequency table is to draw a graph.

Here is the frequency table for the number of goals scored in games involving England, France, Croatia and Switzerland in the 2004 European Championships (we only include the tally column when we are sorting the data).

No. of goals scored	Frequency
0	3
1	2
2	4
3	2
4	1

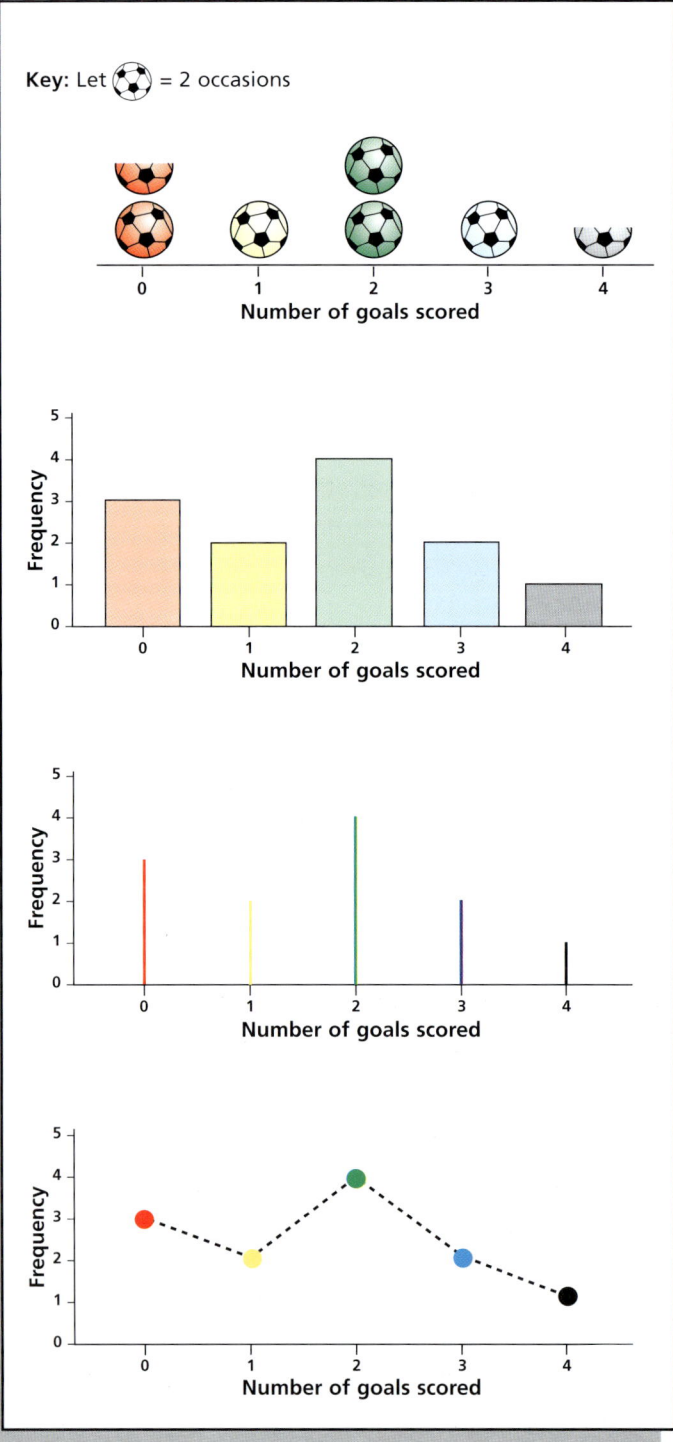

The data above can be displayed in various ways:

A Pictogram

Simple diagrams are used to display data. Since our data is about football we have used a ball. Don't forget to use the key when reading the pictogram.

A Bar Graph

Bars or columns are used to display data. Make sure that the height of each bar is equal to the correct frequency.

A Vertical Line Graph

This graph is very similar to the bar graph above, except that lines are drawn instead of bars. Make sure that the height of each line is equal to the correct frequency.

A Jagged Line Graph

This is not always the most suitable way to display discrete data, as the lines joining the points have no meaning!

Displaying Data 2

Data that has been grouped together and sorted using class intervals into a frequency table can also be displayed by drawing a graph.

Here is the frequency table for the recorded temperatures for various locations at home and abroad.

Recorded temperatures T(°C)	Frequency
10 ⩽ T < 15	2
15 ⩽ T < 20	4
20 ⩽ T < 25	5
25 ⩽ T < 30	8
30 ⩽ T < 35	5

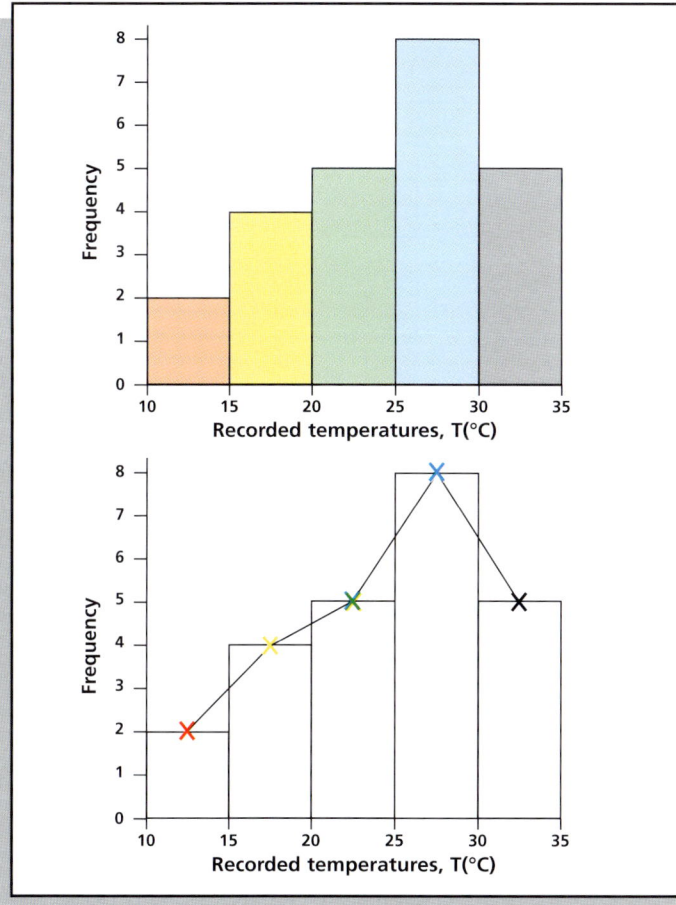

The data above can be displayed in various ways:

A Frequency Diagram

This is very much like a bar graph, but since we have grouped data then the bars do not have a gap between them i.e. they must be continuous, one after another.

A Frequency Polygon

All you need to do is mark the middle of the top of each bar in the frequency diagram with a cross and then join up these crosses with straight lines.

You may be asked to draw a frequency polygon directly from the frequency table. You must remember to plot the crosses at the correct frequency exactly over the middle of the class intervals.

e.g. for **10 ⩽ T < 15**, plot the cross above 12.5

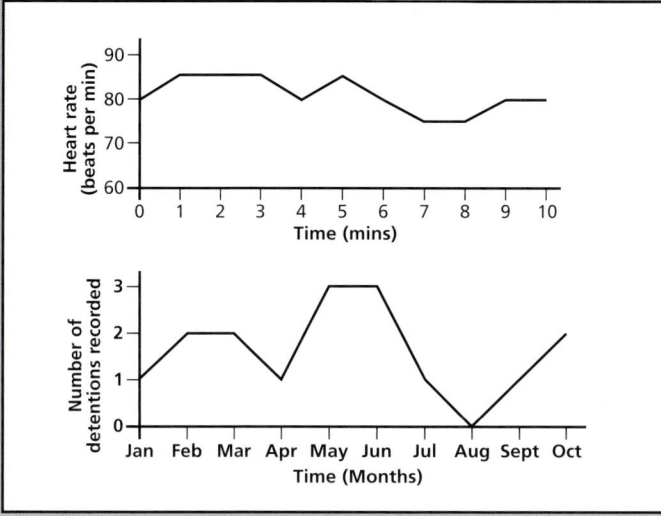

Time Series

One of the most frequently used forms of displaying continuous data involves plotting a line graph of a particular variable against time. This is called a time series. Examples could include:

- The noon temperature in your garden every Sunday
- The daily value of the FTSE 100
- Your height at yearly intervals
- A hardware shop's monthly sales

REMEMBER! In time series graphs, 'Time' is always on the x-axis (horizontal).

Scatter Diagrams 1

A scatter diagram is a graph which has two sets of data plotted on it at the same time. When plotted the points may show a certain trend or correlation. A correlation is defined as the 'strength of relationship between two variables'.

Positive Correlation

As one increases, the other also increases e.g. Number of ice creams sold and daytime temperature.

Negative Correlation

As one increases, the other decreases or vice-versa e.g. Amount of petrol left in tank and distance travelled by car.

Zero Correlation

No obvious trend between the two e.g. Length of hair and height. Remember that zero correlation does not necessarily imply 'no relationship' but merely 'no linear relationship'

Line of Best Fit

This is a straight line that passes through the points so that we have as many points above the line as we have below the line. A line of best fit can only be drawn if our points show positive or negative correlation. Opposite are four different examples of lines of best fit.

A and **B** are **POOR** lines of best fit. They both have the same number of points above and below the line but these points are bunched together and not spread out.

C and **D** are **GOOD** lines of best fit. They both have the same number of points above and below the lines and these points are spread out.

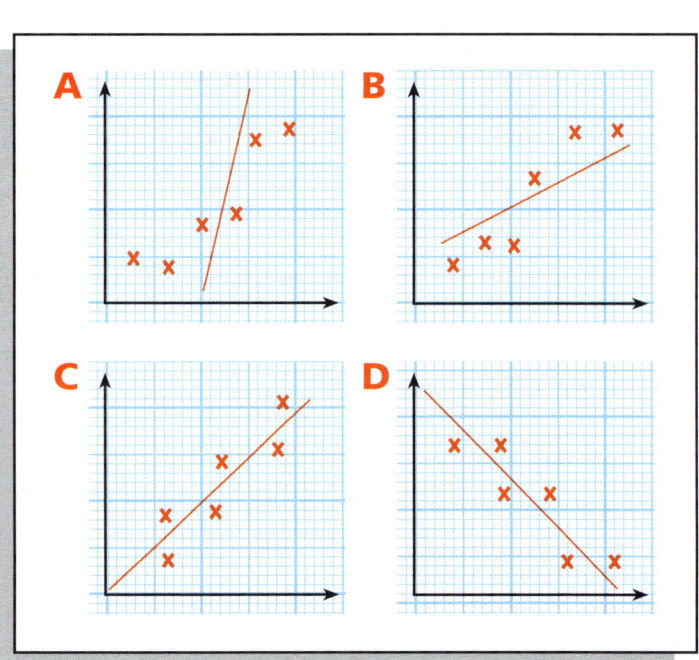

Scatter Diagrams 2

Example

Maths mark	60	30	46	89	48	78	26	38	91	20	65	73
Science mark	56	30	47	98	61	77	38	51	89	25	80	87

The table gives the Maths mark and Science mark for 12 pupils in their end of year examinations.

a) Draw a scatter diagram, including a line of best fit, to show the marks.

b) Tim was absent from his Science exam but he achieved a mark of 65 in his Maths exam. Use your graph to work out an estimated Science mark for Tim.

c) Jenny achieved a mark of 42 in her Science exam but she was absent for her Maths exam. Again use your graph to work out an estimated Maths mark for Jenny.

Solution

a)

The line of best fit doesn't have to pass through the origin (0,0)

The line of best fit doesn't have to pass through any of the points plotted

Your two axes don't have to start from zero. It depends on the numbers you are plotting

b) Go to 65 on the Maths axis and then draw a dotted line ACROSS TO (→) the LINE OF BEST FIT and then DOWN TO (↓) the Science axis. This is Tim's estimated Science mark.

Answer is 70

c) Go to 42 on the Science axis and then draw a dotted line UP TO (↑) the LINE OF BEST FIT and then ACROSS TO (←) the Maths axis. This is Jenny's estimated Maths mark.

Answer is 35

Pie Charts

Drawing Pie Charts

Another way of displaying sorted data is to draw a pie chart. A pie chart is a circle which is split into different sectors. Here are the results of a survey carried out among 18 pupils to find their favourite sport.

Before we can draw our pie chart we need to calculate the ANGLE of the sector representing each sport. To do this we work out the fraction of the pupils for each sport and then multiply this fraction by 360°.

We can now draw our pie chart. Always measure all angles carefully with a protractor and make sure that you always pick the scale on your protractor that starts at 0°.

Favourite Sport	Frequency (no. of pupils)
Football	7
Tennis	3
Hockey	8
	Total = 18

Favourite Sport	Frequency of pupils	Angle to be drawn
Football	Total number of pupils → $\frac{7}{18}$ ← Number who liked football	$\frac{7}{18} \times 360° = 140°$
Tennis	Total number of pupils → $\frac{3}{18}$ ← Number who liked Tennis	$\frac{3}{18} \times 360° = 60°$
Hockey	Total number of pupils → $\frac{8}{18}$ ← Number who liked Hockey	$\frac{8}{18} \times 360° = 160°$
		Total = 360°

1 Pick a starting point and draw a radius

2 Measure and mark 140° for football

3 Measure and mark 60° for tennis

4 Check that the remainder (for hockey) is 160°

5 The completed pie chart will now look like this

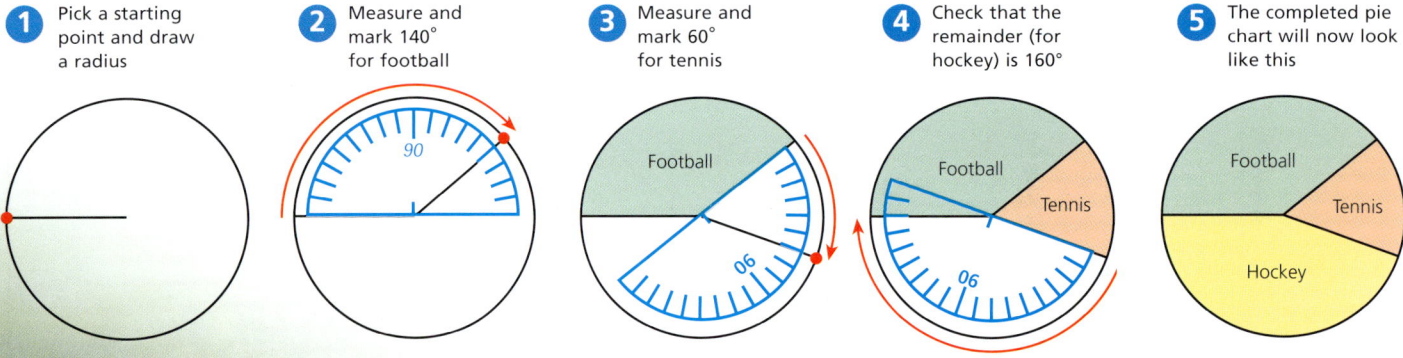

Getting Information from Pie Charts

Getting information from a pie chart is very similar to drawing a pie chart except you need to work backwards. If the pie chart above shows the favourite sport for 18 pupils, the first thing we need to do is measure all the angles. We can then work out the number of pupils for each sport.

Favourite Sport	Fraction of circle	Number of pupils
Football	Total no. of ° for a circle → $\frac{140°}{360°}$ ← Number of ° for football	$\frac{140°}{360°} \times 18 = 7$
Tennis	Total no. of ° for a circle → $\frac{60°}{360°}$ ← Number of ° for tennis	$\frac{60°}{360°} \times 18 = 3$
Hockey	Total no. of ° for a circle → $\frac{160°}{360°}$ ← Number of ° for hockey	$\frac{160°}{360°} \times 18 = 8$
		Total = 18 pupils

Mean, Median, Mode & Range 1

Describing Data

We often use the word 'average' to describe a set of data and this is quite a useful tool. However, two batsmen who both average 35 in five innings could have had the following scores, showing quite different distributions:

Batsman A: 0, 10, 10, 60, 95
Batsman B: 30, 34, 36, 36, 39

In this case the 'average' score doesn't tell us the whole story. For this, we can use three different types of average, Mean, Median and Mode, plus a description of the Range of the data.

Example

Sam has the following coins in his pocket. What he has is a distribution of numbers (the different valued coins).

❶ Mean

This is the AVERAGE value and is given by:

$$\text{Mean} = \frac{\text{SUM OF ALL THE VALUES}}{\text{NUMBER OF VALUES}}$$

$$= \frac{1p+5p+1p+20p+10p+5p+1p+1p+10p}{9 \text{ (number of coins)}}$$

$$= \frac{54p}{9} = \textbf{6p}$$

❷ Median

This is the MIDDLE value, providing that all the numbers have been arranged in order, lowest to highest.

1p, 1p, 1p, 1p, 5p, 5p, 10p, 10p, 20p *Arrange in order*

~~1p~~, ~~1p~~, ~~1p~~, ~~1p~~, 5p, ~~5p~~, ~~10p~~, ~~10p~~, ~~20p~~ *Tick off from the two ends to find the middle value*

Median = 5p

If you tick off from the two ends and are left with two numbers in the middle, then the median is the number halfway between those two numbers (e.g. for ~~1~~, ~~1~~, 1, 2, ~~2~~, ~~2~~ **Median = 1.5**)

❸ Mode

This is the MOST COMMON value i.e. the number that occurs most frequently.

Mode = 1p *1p coin occurs more times than any other coin*

❹ Range

This is the DIFFERENCE between the HIGHEST and the LOWEST value.

Range = 20p - 1p = 19p

Mean, Median, Mode & Range 2

Mean, Median, Mode and Range from a Frequency Table

Here is the frequency table (again) for the number of goals scored in group games involving England, France, Croatia and Switzerland in the 2004 European Championship.

The data in this frequency table is discrete. The same processes would apply if the data was continuous.

Number of goals scored (x)	Frequency (f)	Frequency x no. of goals scored (fx)	
0	3	3 × 0 = 0	← 3 teams have scored 0 goals. Total number of goals scored = 3 × 0 = 0
1	2	2 × 1 = 2	← 2 teams have scored 1 goal. Total number of goals scored = 2 × 1 = 2
2	4	4 × 2 = 8	← 4 teams have scored 2 goals. Total number of goals scored = 4 × 2 = 8
3	2	2 × 3 = 6	← 2 teams have scored 3 goals. Total number of goals scored = 2 × 3 = 6
4	1	1 × 4 = 4	← 1 team has scored 4 goals. Total number of goals scored = 1 × 4 = 4
	Total = 12	Total = 20	← Total number of goals scored. = 0 + 2 + 8 + 6 + 4 = 20

Mean

To calculate the mean we need to add another column (in red) to our frequency table to calculate the total number of goals scored.

$$\text{Mean} = \frac{\text{Total number of goals scored } (fx)}{\text{Total frequency}}$$

$$= \frac{20}{12} = 1.\dot{6} \text{ goals (per team per game)}$$

Mode

Mode = 2 goals

(this occurs more times than any of the others).

> **NOTE:** You may well be asked to identify the modal class from a frequency table involving grouped data (see example on page 84). In the stated example the modal class is **25°C≤T<30°C** since this class interval has the highest frequency (i.e. it occurs the most number of times).

Median

Since we have 12 pieces of data, the median number of goals is halfway between the 6th and 7th piece of data (with an even number you always end up with two numbers in the middle).

3 teams scored	2 teams scored	4 teams scored	2 teams scored	1 team scored
0̸ 0̸ 0̸	1̸ 1̸	②②2̸ 2̸	3̸ 3̸	4̸

$$\text{Median} = \frac{2 + 2}{2}$$
$$= 2 \text{ goals}$$

Range

Range = 4 goals - 0 goals
= 4 goals

Notes

Using a Scientific Calculator 1

Exam Preparation

The Day Before the Exam:
- Check that your calculator is working properly.

Before Entering the Exam:
- Check that your calculator screen is clear.
- Check that the MEMORY is clear.
- Make sure that any FIX, SCI or ENG functions, which may affect your calculations, have been switched off.
- Many calculators have a RESET button on the back. It is a good idea to press this before the exam to restore the basic settings.

*Please note that some calculators may have different operating methods. Please check your own against the examples given.

Using a Scientific Calculator 2

Calculator Function		Example of use	Keys to press
SHIFT or INV or 2nd		**SECOND FUNCTIONS** Press this button to use the 'second functions', which appear on the different buttons of your calculator above the main functions.	
x^2	SQUARE	$5^2 = 25$	5 x^2
$\sqrt{}$	SQUARE ROOT	$\sqrt{49} = 7$	49 $\sqrt{}$ or $\sqrt{}$ 49
x^3	CUBE	$4^3 = 64$	4 x^3 — If you haven't got x^2 and $\sqrt[3]{x}$ keys on your calculator, you can use the x^y, $\sqrt[y]{x}$ and $x^{\frac{1}{y}}$ keys to carry out the same functions.
$\sqrt[3]{x}$	CUBE ROOT	$\sqrt[3]{125} = 5$	125 $\sqrt[3]{x}$
x^y	POWER	$4^6 = 4096$	4 x^y 6
$x^{\frac{1}{y}}$ or $\sqrt[y]{x}$	ROOT	$\sqrt[4]{6561} = 9$	6561 $x^{\frac{1}{y}}$ 4 or 4 $x^{\frac{1}{y}}$ 6561
Min MR	MEMORY	Finally get used to using the memory buttons. Min stores a number (usually the answer to a calculation) in the calculator's memory. MR is used to recall the number when needed e.g. as part of a related calculation.	
$a^{b/c}$	FRACTION	To key in $2\frac{3}{5}$	2 $a^{b/c}$ 3 $a^{b/c}$ 5
d/c		Press d/c to convert keyed-in mixed number into an improper fraction. Press $a^{b/c}$ again to convert improper fraction into a decimal.	
[(... ...)]	BRACKETS	$(5 + 2) \times 6 = 42$	[(... 5 + 2 ...)] × 6 =

Index

A
Acute Angles 44
Addition 6, 8, 16, 19
Algebra 30-43
Allied Angles 45
Alternate Angles 45
Angles 44-46, 48-50
Arcs 76
Area 61-63
Axes 38

B
Bar Graphs 86
Bearings 70
Bidmas 9, 31
Brackets 9, 32, 95

C
Charts 27
Checking Answers 12
Chords 76
Circles 60, 63, 76
Circumference 60, 76
Class Intervals 84
Collecting Data 81-82
Common Factors 5
Comparisons 24
Compound Shapes 63
Congruence 51
Constructions 74-75
Continuous Data 83
Conversion Graphs 42
Conversions 72
Coordinates 38-40, 57-58
Correlation 89
Corresponding Angles 45
Credit 16
Cube Numbers 13, 95
Cube Roots 95
Cuboids 64-66

D
Data 81-93
Decimal Places 10
Decimals 18-21, 25
Diameter 60, 76
Discrete Data 83
Displaying Data 86-88
Distance-Time Graphs 43
Division 6, 8, 16, 21

E
Elevations 66
Enlargements 56
Equilateral Triangles 47
Equivalent Fractions 14
Estimated Probability 80
Estimating Answers 12
Estimating Area 61
Even Numbers 5
Everyday Maths 26-27
Exams 94
Expressions 30

F
Factorisation 32
Factors 5
Formulae 35-36
Fractions 14-17, 25, 28, 95
Frequency Diagram 87
Frequency Polygon 87
Frequency Tables 83-84, 92

G
Graphs 39-43, 86-87

H
Hexagons 49-50, 75
Household Bills 27

I
Identities 30
Imperial Units 72
Improper Fractions 15
Integers 7-8
Interest 26
Irregular Polygons 49
Isometric Paper 65
Isosceles Triangles 47

J
Jagged Line Graphs 86

K
Kites 48

L
Like Terms 30
Line of Best Fit 88-89
Linear Equations 33-34
Linear Functions 39-40
Lines of Symmetry 67

M
Map Scales 69
Mean 91-92
Median 91-92
Memory Keys 95
Metric Units 72
Mixed Numbers 15
Mode 91-92
Money 18
Multiples 5
Multiplication 6, 8, 16, 20

N
Nets 66
Number Patterns 37

O
Obtuse Angles 44
Odd Numbers 5
Origin 38
Outcomes 78-79

P
Parallel Lines 45
Parallelograms 48
Pentagons 49-50
Percentages 22-25
Perimeter 59-60
Pictograms 86
Pie Charts 90
Place Value 4, 18
Plane Symmetry 66
Plans 66
Plotting Points 38
Polygons 49
Powers 13, 95
Primary Data 81
Probability 77-80
Proportion 28-29

Q
Quadrants 38
Quadrilaterals 48
Quantities 17, 21, 29
Questionnaires 82

R
Radius 60, 76
Range 91-92
Ratio 28-29
Reading Scales 71
Reciprocals 5
Rectangles 48
Recurring Decimals 19
Reflections 53
Reflective Symmetry 67
Reflex Angles 44
Regular Polygons 50
Rhombuses 48
Right-Angled Triangles 47
Right-Angles 44
Roots 13, 95
Rotational Symmetry 68
Rotations 54
Rounding Numbers 4, 10-11

S
Sampling 81
Scale Drawings 69
Scale Factor 56
Scalene Triangles 47
Scatter Diagrams 88-89
Scientific Calculators 94-95
Second Functions 95
Secondary Data 81
Sequences 37
Significant Figures 11
Similarity 52
Solids 65
Sorting Data 83-85
Speed 43, 73
Square Numbers 13, 95
Square Roots 13, 95
Squares 48
Stem and Leaf Diagrams 85
Substitution 31
Subtraction 6, 8, 16, 19
Surface Area 63
Symmetry 66-68

T
Tables 27, 85
Tally Charts 83-84
Tangents 76
Terminating Decimals 19
Tessellation 51
Theoretical Probability 80
Three-Dimensional Shapes 66
Three-Figure Bearings 70
Times Series 87
Transformations 53-56
Translations 55
Trapeziums 48
Triangles 46-47, 74
Two Way Tables 85

V
VAT 26
Vertical Line Graphs 86
Vertically Opposite Angles 44
Volume 64